Understanding Suicidal Behaviour

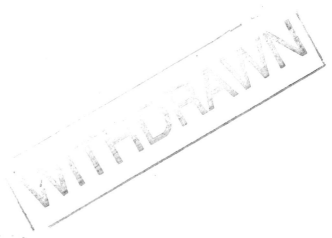

Dr Michael Kelleher (1937–1998), for his contribution to the field of suicide research

Mr Ciaran O'Connor (1945–1996), my father (R. O'Connor)

Understanding Suicidal Behaviour

Rory O'Connor
Noel Sheehy

BPS Blackwell

Editorial Offices:
108 Cowley Road, Oxford OX4 1JF, UK
    Tel: +44 (0)1865 791100
350 Main Street, Malden, MA 02148-5018, USA
    Tel: +1 781 388 8250

First published 2000 by The British Psychological Society
A BPS Blackwell book

Library of Congress Cataloging-in-Publication Data has been applied for

ISBN 1 85433 290 2

A catalogue record for this title is available from the British Library.

Set by Book Production Services, London
Printed and bound in Great Britain by MPG Books Ltd, Bodmin, Cornwall

For further information on
Blackwell Publishers, visit our website:
www.blackwellpublishers.co.uk

Contents

Preface

The traditional view of suicide as profoundly unusual is challenged by the fact that suicide and attempted suicide are the largest causes of death and injury to young adults. Suicide is everywhere. It can have an insidious influence on the families and friends of those who have taken their own lives.

There are no quick and easy solutions to the complex problem of suicide, but a starting point is to consider how we respond to emotional distress in ourselves and in the people we see around us. This book aims to de-mystify suicide and show how regarding suicide as the product of an insane mind fails to explain why people kill themselves and how those considering suicide may be helped. Written in a jargon-free style and from a theoretically eclectic position, it examines the social and intellectual origins of the view that suicide is profoundly abnormal and a case for medical treatment.

Commencing with a history of suicide, we trace the origins of contemporary theories and attitudes towards suicide. Through an analysis of suicide letters and conversations with those who have recently attempted suicide, we show how an understanding of suicidal communication can enlighten our thinking. The book explores motives for suicide and listens to people talk about what has happened to them.

Understanding suicide leads to the most challenging task – predicting when someone will kill themselves. Approaches to the early detection of suicide are examined and implications for prevention are considered. The ethics of intervening, or failing to intervene, are considered in the context of the needs and rights of those who consider the suicide option.

This is a review book, aimed at a variety of readers, from undergraduates through postgraduates to medical professionals and people with an interest in understanding suicidal behaviour. Chapter 1 begins with an historical perspective, highlighting the social and cultural influences on suicidal behaviour. The second chapter is concerned with the problems of measurement and the difficulties encountered in carrying out research in this field. The risk factors (clinical, social and person factors) are reviewed in the subsequent three chapters. In the second half of the book, we deal with suicide communication in terms of suicide notes (Chapter 6) and parasuicides (Chapter 7). Here we address, in detail, the insights that can be gained from studying suicide sub-types, thoughts and actions. The penultimate chapter looks at the controversial issue of assisted suicide (Chapter 8) and the last chapter addresses strategies and developments, both global and specific, germane to suicide prevention (Chapter 9).

Acknowledgements

Many thanks to our family and friends who supported us during this project, and read drafts of chapters. Particular appreciation to Suzy Harper, Derek Heim, Raymond MacDonald, Catherine O'Connor, Daryl O'Connor, Jonathan Smallwood, Wendy Sheehy and the anonymous reviewers.

1

Suicide in the History of Western Civilization

'There is but one truly serious philosophical problem, and that is suicide. Judging whether life is or is not worth living amounts to answering the fundamental questions of philosophy.'
(Albert Camus, *The Myth of Sisyphus*, p.11)

How have we developed our ideas about the meaning of suicide and what should be done about this way of dying? Attitudes to suicide have a rich and complex history. Western civilization has at different times regarded the act as virtuous, or as a crime against society and/or a violation of God's law. Contemporary views on suicide do not exist in a historical vacuum, but in researching the history of suicide it is important to be wary of inadvertently projecting current language, ideas and interpretations on the perspectives of earlier periods. For example, the word 'suicide' has a relatively recent history; the first recorded use is attributed to Sir Thomas Browne's 1634 account of the death of Cato. The term was sufficiently obscure not to appear in Dr Johnson's *Dictionary* of 1755. Only 250 years ago the phrases more· commonly used to refer to suicide were 'self-slaughter', 'self-killing' and 'self-destruction', all of which carried strong connotations of murderous behaviour (Alvarez, 1971).

Conversely, we should be aware that contemporary Western attitudes towards death and dying would strike even our relatively recent forebears as somewhat peculiar. In the early and middle part of the 20th century death was public, simple and commonplace, and a century ago considerably more conspicuous in childhood experiences than it is today. Partly because there were fewer opportunities to restrict children's contact with death, the sight of death and the dead was much more familiar to young children. Contemporary values and practices favour sheltering children from death, delaying for example, for as long as possible, the first sight of a human corpse. To the Greek and Roman societies of 2000 years ago our social manners and customs surrounding death would seem as strange and puzzling as our view of their attitudes and rituals sometimes seem to us.

Attitudes of the Greeks and Romans

The pre-Christian Roman and early Greek civilizations are widely considered to have embraced an exceptionally tolerant attitude to suicide. That attitude, however, developed from an earlier hostile view that likened self-killing to the slaughter of family members. Indeed early Greek language does not draw a clear distinction between murder of kin and 'self-murder'. Nonetheless, analyses of more than a thousand suicides recorded in ancient histories and dramas, from inscriptions on tombs and on papyri suggest that when suicide was reported it was done with a matter-of-factness that warranted neither extended commentary nor moral censure (Van Hooff, 1994).

The ancient Greeks normally took their lives for the most worthy of reasons: grief, patriotic principle or to avoid the shame of dishonour. Suicide could attract condemnation if it were done for lesser motives, such as disrespect to the gods or cowardice. Thus, in classical Greece suicide was tolerated provided it was reasoned and reasonable, and Stoic philosophers developed this view to a point where the act was regarded as the ideal death entirely in accordance with natural law. For example, in the *Phaedo* the condemned Socrates argues that he should accept death since he will attain the greatest blessings in the next life, and he urges other philosophers to follow his example. Thus many Stoics, inspired by his arguments that death is a rational choice reflecting the intrinsically rational order of nature, took their own lives and were praised for so doing.

The Romans adopted a similar view, looking on suicide with neither fear nor moral revulsion but rather as a validation of how they had lived and the principles by which they had lived. Dignity, bravery and style were values deeply embedded in the Roman psyche and the manner of one's demise was a practical, public expression of a person's commitment to these high virtues. In that context, suicide was regarded as reasonable and eminently virtuous. Of course within the broader Roman perspective certain kinds of suicide – suicide for entirely irrational reasons – attracted condemnation, as did suicide among slaves. One reason for outlawing certain types of suicide was the high incidence among slaves who, by taking their own lives, deprived their owners of valuable property. Suicide among soldiers was outlawed for much the same reason: they were regarded as the property of the state and suicide was tantamount to desertion.

Early Christian writers

The early Christians took over Roman religious festivals and transformed them, and in much the same way they embraced Roman attitudes to death and suicide. For Christians life was relatively unimportant, a temporal phase full of temptations to sin that could significantly affect entry to Paradise. Thus, death was regarded as a long-awaited release to the next life that could be expedited through suicide. Commentators, such as Tertullian, regarded the death of Jesus as suicide through martyrdom (Alvarez, 1971) and for some Christians the distinction between suicide and martyrdom was more than a little blurred. This is probably best reflected in the lifestyles of the Donatists, a sect based in North Africa whose zeal for martyrdom, and the promise of redemption through suicide, was so extreme it forced the early Church to condemn their actions as heresy.

The early Christian enthusiasm for suicide through martyrdom posed a significant problem for the church. Suicide is rarely mentioned in the Old Testament which describes just six acts, none attracting comment or condemnation. In Judg. 9:54, Abimelech, wounded during a battle by a woman who threw a stone at his head, is reported to have commanded his armour-bearer to kill him rather than endure the shame of being killed by a woman. In Judg. 16:26–31, Samson brought the Philistine temple at Gaza down on his head after being blinded but was considered to have died honourably by delivering God's justice on the Philistines. In 1 Sam. 31:1–4, Saul attempted to avoid capture by ordering his armour-bearer to kill him. When the latter refused Saul killed himself with his own sword, and his armour-bearer died in a similar fashion in order to be equal in service to his master (1 Sam. 31:5). Ahitophel, who had been royal adviser to David before he joined David's rebellious son Absalom, killed himself by hanging when Absalom refused to take his advice (2 Sam. 17:23). Finally, Zimiri, who led an unsuccessful rebellion against King Elah of Israel, avoided capture by entombing himself in his own palace (Kings 16:18).

St Augustine recognized the dilemma in Christian teaching: if the Old Testament did not condemn suicide, if baptism removed all sin, and if suicide were allowed in order to avoid sin and hasten eternal life, then suicide, ideally through martyrdom, could become the obvious choice for Christian converts. In addressing this problem Augustine embraced and reworked the philosophy of Plato and the Pythorageans. They had previously argued that life is God's will, that to take one's life involved rejecting God's will and therefore suicide should be judged as profoundly sinful. Another of Augustine's revisions was to reinterpret the Sixth Commandment, 'Thou shalt not kill', in ways that echoed the view of early Greek civilization, namely that killing oneself was no different from murdering others in one's family.

It was against this background, the challenge presented by the desire for martyrdom, that St Augustine condemned all killing and prompted the Church to legislate against suicide. Thus, in 533 the Council of Orleans outlawed suicide and denied funeral rites to all who killed themselves. In 562 the Council of Braga refused funeral rites to all suicides regardless of their motive or social position; later, in 693, the Council of Toledo ruled that anyone who *attempted* suicide should be excommunicated.

St Thomas Aquinas sought to make Augustine's thesis more systematic and scientific by drawing on the ideas of Aristotle. Aquinas (1929) outlined three reasons why suicide should be regarded as a mortal sin. First, it was contrary to natural law because everything in nature resists corruption and death for as long as it can; suicide was an affront to natural law. Second, since every part belongs to a whole, and since every individual is part of society, suicide deprives society, the whole, of something which belongs to it. Third, human life is given by God and suicide is therefore a sin against God.

Later attitudes towards suicide

The Christian Church's view of suicide remained largely unaltered for several hundred years and was only substantially modified by writers and philosophers during the 1500s. For example, Shakespeare comments on the practice of denying full burial rites to those who chose suicide:

> *She should in ground unsanctified have lodged*
> *Till the last trumpet; for charitable prayers,*
> *Shards, flints, and pebbles should be thrown on her.*
> (*Hamlet*, Act 5, Scene 1)

The poet John Donne published (posthumously in 1644) 'Biathanatos' in which he argued that suicide was not necessarily incompatible with the laws of God and could be justifiable. Similarly, the philosopher David Hume (1711–1776) did not regard suicide as sinful and in his 'On Suicide' argued that 'prudence and courage should engage us to rid ourselves at once of existence when it becomes a burden'. Others, such as Immanuel Kant (1724–1804), disagreed and argued for a more traditional view based on the sacredness of human life.

Although the 16th and 17th centuries are associated with a more tolerant view of suicide, the act was still regarded as a profound threat to both spiritual and secular order. For example, the French Criminal

Ordinance (1670, August) required the body of a suicide to be dragged through the streets and dumped. Suicide was decriminalized (1789) in France soon after the French Revolution, but much later (1961) in the UK and the Republic of Ireland (1993)

The high Roman attitude to suicide was not uniformly embraced. There can be little doubt that slaves and many of those persecuted for their religious beliefs took their own lives to escape their intolerable circumstances. The possibility that social forces could shape suicidal behaviour was explored by Jean-Jacques Rousseau (1712–1778) who took the view that society should bear much of the responsibility for so-called individual acts of evil. His definition of suicide as a social problem with medical and sociological implications prompted Lachaise (1822) to investigate suicide in Paris and to conclude that the origins and incidence of suicide were mostly concealed because of the stigma and distress caused to the family. The work of Lachaise and others (Casper, 1825, Falret, 1822 and Spurzheim, 1818) transformed the study of suicide from being an exclusively ethical subject into a medical one, and provoked demands for fuller explanations rather than moral condemnation. Brierre de Boismont (1856) was probably the first to conclude that suicide could be caused by alcoholism, mental illness, poverty and related social factors.

Psychology of suicide

Psychological theories of suicide are developed within a wider social, religious and political context and are founded on broadly based cultural value systems. Consequently, a historical perspective on psychological approaches to suicide reflects wider cultural influences and tensions. For example, notwithstanding a more liberal and humanitarian attitude to suicide, the behaviour is widely regarded as fundamentally abnormal and psychology locates suicide firmly within the subdivision of abnormal psychology.

Treating suicide as fundamentally abnormal involves, first, making comparisons with other people's behaviour and, second, interpreting the consequences for others of the behaviour in question. Thus, suicide has been regarded, within psychology and more generally, as not behaving, feeling or thinking as one should. Norms are concerned with what is 'right', 'proper' or 'natural', and suicidal behaviour has often been regarded as an unacceptable breach of these norms. But 'unacceptable' to whom? There are tensions within psychology which raise doubts about the value of defining suicide in this way and these are mirrored in different criteria that have been used to confine suicide to the realm of the abnormal.

Statistical definitions of abnormal behaviour

The statistical definition of abnormal behaviour is essentially quantitative, based on the frequency with which a particular behaviour can be observed in the general population. On this criterion, infrequent behaviour, such as suicide, counts as abnormal. However, a statistical definition poses three problems. First, it is not clear how far from the population average or how unusual any kind of behaviour must be to be considered abnormal. For example, should the cut-off point be one standard deviation above or below the mean, or two, or three standard deviations? The choice of cut-off point is arbitrary.

Second, deviations from the population average are almost always evaluated unequally. Someone who wishes to live forever, on a strict statistical criterion, might be considered just as 'abnormal' as someone who longs to be dead. However, these two desires are not usually regarded as equally 'abnormal', suggesting that a statistical definition of abnormality does not fully capture what is conveyed by the description of suicidal behaviour as abnormal. What we seem to be looking for is a definition that captures behaviour that is 'abnormally bad'– whatever that means – and a statistical definition does not do this.

Third, statistical criteria assume that psychological characteristics in general can be viewed as *dimensional* (e.g. as in *Diagnostic and Statistical Manual of Mental Disorders*, DSM-IV). Everyone can be placed somewhere on the dimension according to their scores on tests and questionnaires. In reality it is often extremely difficult to construct dimensions for many kinds of very important behaviours – friendship, honesty, love, trust, regret and so on – that are fundamental to our social and personal interactions with others and that are known to be implicated in many acts of suicide.

Suicide as unexpected behaviour

Behaviour that is considered unexpected might be a criterion for defining suicide as abnormal, but it is difficult to determine what counts as unexpected behaviour. Behaviour that might be judged unexpected by one person may be regarded as entirely expected by another. The family and friends of those who have killed themselves often describe the act as completely unexpected. However, a coroner's enquiry might uncover diaries and letters that indicate how the final outcome could be regarded as completely expected given the newly discovered evidence of the person's thoughts and feelings about the quality of his or her life. Moreover, many kinds of behaviour, such as day-dreaming or yawning, can be considered unexpected but we would not wish to count them as abnormal. The unexpectedness criterion does not define which behaviours are intrinsically important in determining abnormality and which are not. One might think that the unexpected behaviour criterion is essentially to do with behaviours that are out of all proportion to the situation, but that begs two questions: who is to decide, and by how much must something be 'in proportion'? With hindsight we can sometimes see how suicide, for example by someone terminally ill, was chosen as a proportionate solution to an unendurable and inescapable situation.

Suicide as inconsistent behaviour

Abnormality is sometimes judged with reference to the degree of internal consistency in a person's behaviour. Abnormal behaviour is often characterized by contradictions and inconsistencies of a kind observed in suicidal thoughts and feelings. However, human beings are usually inconsistent and an assessment of the degree of inconsistency is as much a reflection of the perspective of the person making the judgement as it is of the person whose behaviour is being judged. Moreover, whereas highly inconsistent behaviour would certainly count as erratic, there are many harmless eccentrics who we would not want to count as abnormal or a risk to themselves. Furthermore, it is important to keep in mind that well-concealed plans for suicide almost always succeed because the deceased possessed the self-control to behave 'normally'– consistently and coherently – with those around them and had the insight to see their wishes through in a fashion unnoticed by those around them.

Suicide as personal distress

At one time or another we all think about how we may die and experience a normal sense of unease and concern. Using a different criterion we could define as abnormal those suicidal feelings and thoughts that cause us deep personal distress. Many of those who think about killing themselves endure seemingly unbearable psychological pain, but this isn't true of everyone. Some disorders, for example psychoses, are characterized by both lack of insight and an absence of personal distress and therefore would not satisfy this criterion. Moreover, there are many instances of planned suicide, for example among the terminally ill, which appear to be guided by a reflective, insightful analysis that Stoic philosophy would regard as rational, virtuous, spiritual and dignified.

Others' distress

Throughout history the distress of others has strongly influenced definitions of abnormality. What we count as abnormal behaviour can certainly cause stress and distress in others, but the perceptions and behaviours of others can be biased and irrational and lead to stereotypes of 'suicidal madness'. The 'others' distress criterion' drives our desire to define, explain and remedy suicidal behaviour in those around us. In this sense a psychological perspective on suicide as 'abnormal' is the product of complex interpersonal processes – it is fundamentally to do with our relationships with one another – not just aberrant intrapersonal, intrapsychic processes 'all in the head' of supposedly deranged people.

Suicide as maladaptive

We might say that abnormal behaviour is essentially behaviour that is not adaptive – it is not in the interests of the person because suicide is a permanent solution to an ephemeral or temporary problem. This would seem to be a very powerful criterion. For example, high levels of anxiety, abuse of alcohol and self-injurious behaviour would count as suicidal, maladaptive and abnormal behaviour. However, even this criterion is problematic. Consider a 15-year-old girl diagnosed as suffering from anorexia nervosa who regularly cuts herself and from time to time makes a serious attempt to take her own life. This seems profoundly maladaptive and not in the best interests of the girl. Suppose we discover that the girl has been systematically abused both physically and sexually. In that context her behaviour could be considered highly adaptive: it is so extreme that she gets noticed by medical and social welfare professionals, the police and the criminal justice system, who can apply considerable resources to help her change her life circumstances. Sometimes ostensibly maladaptive behaviour may be to the longer term advantage of the person.

Conclusion

The history of suicide in Western civilization is marked by a number of radical changes. Early Greek society promoted a tolerant view that was embraced by the Romans who extolled the virtues of suicide motivated by high principles. Early Christians adopted suicide with a fervour that prompted the Church to reinterpret the act with intense moral revulsion. The counter-revolution of science, and social science, sought to replace moral outrage and social stigma with a more 'enlightened' view. The suicidal person was no longer regarded as morally corrupt, nor a criminal, but rather as a victim of hostile social forces inducing abnormal psychological processes. Within this enlightened view suicide is, nevertheless, rejected as abnormal – as psychologically bad and socially problematic. We may feel that, notwithstanding problems of definition, this view is broadly correct, but it should not be adopted unquestioningly nor should it be taken as the legitimate view. If we think uncritically of suicide as essentially abnormal we run the risk of labelling the suicidal person as an undignified tragedy. Paradoxically the secularization and destigmatization of suicide recapitulates the forbearance of early Western civilization and by implication makes available a way of dying that might otherwise be rejected. Our renewed tolerance for suicide carries with it the possibility that an unknown number of people who might otherwise have rejected suicide on moral grounds, or fear for the stigma that would befall their families, will more readily embrace this way of dying.

Chapter review

- Pre-Christian Roman and early Greek civilizations adopted a tolerant attitude to suicide which was embraced by the early Christians and posed dilemmas for the early Church.
- The systematic criminalization and stigmatization of suicide can be traced to the sixth century AD and was largely unchallenged for a thousand years.
- The Enlightment produced the first modern secularized theories of ethics and psychology, and prompted a rational, systematic examination of the determinants and correlates of suicide.
- Theories of suicide are not formulated in a social and moral vacuum and contemporary psychological perspectives continue to treat suicidal thought and action as profoundly abnormal.
- Psychological definitions of suicide expose aspects of competing moral influences and social forces that shape this perspective.
- Paradoxically, increased tolerance and understanding of suicide may encourage a greater number of people to consider suicide as a way to solve their problems.

2
Issues of Definition, Incidence and Measurement

To understand suicidal behaviour we must first define it, recognize its prevalence and identify the methods employed to measure it. That is, what is it? How often does it occur? And how do we know it occurs? Like many aspects of human existence, suicidal behaviour is defined culturally as well as scientifically. However, for us to get at all close to an understanding of why people kill themselves, we must be aware, at the very least, of the biases and limitations of defining this behaviour and, at the very best, we must agree on what unequivocally characterizes this phenomenon.

Defining the issue

How is suicidal behaviour defined?

Suicidal behaviour incorporates a wide variety of behaviours that involve the intention of or actual self-harm, ranging from suicidal thoughts and gestures through to self-harm, attempted suicide and completed suicide. There is no universally agreed definition of suicide or attempted suicide and differences exist regarding whether an individual actually intended to commit suicide. This makes comparative analysis of national suicide statistics problematic and unreliable. In recent decades, however, a certain degree of consensus has been reached.

Intuitively, suicide involves the *intentional* taking of one's life; the difficulty lies in determining this intent. Diekstra (1994) defined suicide as a 'self-chosen behaviour that is intended to bring about one's own death in the short(est) term'. Others view suicide as being multidimensional and the solution to a perceived problem: 'suicide is a conscious act of self-induced annihilation, best understood as a multidimensional malaise in a needful individual who defines an issue for which suicide is perceived as the best solution' (Shneidman, 1985, p.22). The bereaved often see suicide as a permanent solution to a temporary problem.

Many terms have been used to describe behaviour that entails putting one's life at risk: attempted suicide, self-injurious behaviour, deliberate self-harm and parasuicide. Most researchers in Europe prefer parasuicide to refer to any non-accidental act of self-injury that does not result in death. It is favoured because we do not have to make any assumptions about the individual's intention. It encompasses those who, at the time of the episode, did *and* did not want to die. Norman Kreitman coined the term parasuicide in the 1970s to cover all behaviours that involve self-injury, including manipulative behaviours and genuine attempts to end one's own life (Kreitman, 1976). Parasuicide is 'a non-fatal act in which an individual deliberately causes self-injury or ingests a substance in excess of any prescribed or generally recognized therapeutic dosage' (Kreitman, 1977). This definition makes no reference to the individual's intent and in many ways is at odds with how suicide is commonly defined. Kreitman argues that the establishment of intent should not be used as a defining criterion because the retrospective inferring of intention is incredibly complex and fraught with technical difficulties.

'Parasuicide' is not the dominant expression in North America where, for the most part, researchers still use 'attempted suicide' (e.g. Spirito et al., 1996) to describe intentional self-injury. That said, there is some movement towards embracing an all-encompassing terminology. For the purposes here, parasuicide, attempted suicide, deliberate self-harm and self-injury are used interchangeably.

An attempt at consensus

In March 1997, the International Association for Suicide Prevention (IASP) held its biannual congress in Adelaide, Australia. The theme of the congress was 'Suicide Prevention: the Global Context'. One outcome was the proposal of a nomenclature for suicidology – general definitions for suicide-related behaviours. This was developed, through numerous workshops and discussions over several years, and finally written up recently by several prominent suicidologists (O'Carroll et al., 1998). Here the authors make the distinction between nomenclature and classification: nomenclature is a collection of commonly defined terms, whereas the goal of a classification system is to establish something that is aetiologically and therapeutically valid. They argue that although a comprehensive classification system is difficult to develop, we need to start sometime – so, why not now? Further, an agreed nomenclature would promote effective communication between researchers, clinicians and victims alike, as well as

11

stimulating discussion and research that will aid the development of a predictive classification scheme.

The proposed nomenclature for suicide and self-injurious thoughts and behaviours

This is a parsimonious system that takes account of the difficulties already outlined (e.g. determination of intention). It is based on the three central elements set out in the Operational Criteria for the Determination of Suicide: outcome, self-infliction and intent to kill oneself (OCDS; Rosenberg et al., 1988). In other words, what was the outcome? Death, injury or no injury? Was the episode self-inflicted? Yes or no? And was their intention to (a) kill oneself or (b) to use the idea of suicide to manipulate one's own situation? This nomenclature goes further than the OCDS and takes fuller account of intention and accidental occurrences (see Table 2.1)

Table 2.1 An outline indicating superset/subset relationships of the proposed nomenclature for suicide and self-injurious thoughts and behaviours

I. Self-injurious thoughts and behaviours
   A. Risk-taking thoughts and behaviours
      1. with immediate risk (e.g. motorcycling, skydiving)
      2. with remote risk (e.g. smoking, sexual promiscuity*)*

   B. Suicide-related thoughts and behaviours
      1. Suicide ideation
         a. Casual ideation
         b. Serious ideation
           (1) persistent
           (2) transient
      2. Suicide-related behaviours
         a. Instrumental suicide-related behaviour (ISRB)
           (1) Suicide threat
               (a) passive (e.g. ledge-sitting)
              (b) active (e.g. verbal threat, note-writing)
           (2) Other ISRB
           (3) Accidental death associated with ISRB
         b. Suicidal acts
           (1) Suicide attempt
               (a) with no injuries (e.g. gun fired but missed)
              (b) with injuries
           (2) Suicide (completed suicide)

Source: Kosky, Eshkevari et al. (1998)

Suicide is defined as 'death from injury, poisoning, or suffocation where there is evidence (either explicit or implicit) that the injury was self-inflicted and that the decedent intended to kill himself/herself (OCDS definition)' (in O'Carroll et al., 1998, p.32). These definitions distinguish between engaging in a self-injurious act with (1) the intention of death (suicide-related behaviour) and (2) without intention to die (instrumental suicide-related behaviour). Suicidal ideation is defined as 'any self-reported thoughts of engaging in suicide-related behaviour' (ibid, p.34).

Cases 2.1 and 2.2 illustrate the utility of this nomenclature.

Case 2.1

HB is a 37-year-old mother of two children. She is living on income support and in the last six months has been admitted several times to her local Accident and Emergency Department presenting with self-poisoning. On each occasion she denies suicidal motives, saying that she took one paracetamol too many and should not drink (alcohol) *as much as she does. For the past year she has been living in sheltered accommodation and has tried unsuccessfully to get her own State-maintained flat. She believes that by harming herself she has a better chance of getting accommodation for herself and her children.*

Case 2.2

WE was 39 years of age, divorced and did not have access to his three children. He worked as a bank clerk and seemed quite happy at work. His general practitioner had him diagnosed as being mildly depressive but he had never exhibited any suicidal behaviours. He had never talked about suicidal thoughts nor, to the best of the GP's knowledge, had he ever tried to harm himself. On New Year's Eve, a gunshot was heard from his house, but when the police came to investigate he denied any knowledge of the incident. One week later he was admitted with self-poisoning by paraquat. He subsequently died. When checking his house his mother discovered one suicide note, dated 31 December.

HB did not want to kill herself, but wanted a flat for herself and her family. She failed to realize that her actions could have had two possible outcomes: (i) relocation to a new flat and/or (ii) her children placed in care by the social services. She seemed unaware of the latter option. In terms of suicidal behaviour, the self-poisoning was an act of self-injury, but motivated not necessarily by a death wish but by social concerns. This is an example of *suicide-related behaviour: instrumental suicidal behaviour*, defined as 'potentially self-injurious behaviour for which there is evidence (either implicit or explicit) that (a) the person did not intend to kill himself/herself (i.e. had zero intent to die) and (b) the person wished to use the appearance of intending to kill himself/herself in order to attain some other end' (O'Carroll et al., 1998, p. 34).

Conversely, WE intended to kill himself on both occasions. The first incident, the gunshot, would not have been classified as a suicidal act without the suicide note. Sadly, he succeeded in his intention one week later. The gunshot incident is an example of *suicidal acts: suicide attempt with no injuries*.

Patrick O'Carroll and colleagues hope that, at the very least, their system will act as a catalyst to others. Researchers and clinicians alike should give some thought to this nomenclature and identify its strengths and weaknesses. In this way, we will edge closer to its operationalization and implementation. To this end, we have started to classify deliberate self-harm patients according to this procedure, with little, if any, difficulty. It is well thought out and seems to take account of all conceived eventualities. However, research has yet to determine whether this type of classification system is any more effective than those we currently employ in predicting prospective suicides and suicide-related behaviours. Without such a schema, studies of 21st century suicides will be dogged by the same methodological concerns as in previous decades, unable to compare studies confidently, or communicate with each other effectively about this global phenomenon.

The prevalence of suicide: collecting and analysing the data

Contemporary interest in suicide is a reflection of rising trends in suicide rates in many countries around the world. After accidents and homicides, the suicide rate among adolescents is reported to be the third leading cause of death (Blumenthal, 1990). In Australia, suicide is now the leading cause of death ahead of car accidents and homicide (Baume and McTaggart, 1998). Suicide rates have also been rising in England and Wales (Hawton, 1992), Scotland (Crombie, 1990b), Northern Ireland (McCrea, 1996) and the Irish Republic (Kelleher and Daly, 1990). In England and Wales there was a large fall in suicides during the 1960s, probably due to the substitution of natural gas for coal gas which made suicide by domestic gas almost impossible (Kreitman, 1976). Since then, the suicide rates have increased for men and have decreased slightly for women (Crombie, 1990b). In 1990, the suicide rates for men and women were 14.8 and 7 per 100,000 respectively (Pollock, 1993).

There has been a steady increase in suicide rates among men aged between 15 and 44 since the mid-1970s. A comparable increase has not been observed for women. In Scotland, during the 1960s, the decline in suicide rates among men was smaller than that reported for the rest of the UK and there was little change in the rate for women. While the rate for men increased considerably throughout the 1970s and 1980s, the rate for women has remained about the same. Rates for men increased by over 40 per cent between 1974–1976 and 1982–1984, while rates for women show a small decrease over the same time period (McLoone and Crombie, 1987). The rates of suicide in Northern Ireland over a 70-year period (1922–1992) show the greatest increase in suicide within the population of young males aged 34 years and younger (McCrea, 1996). In the Republic of Ireland there was a sevenfold increase in suicide throughout the 1970s and early 1980s from 1.75 per 100,000 in 1979 to 7.87 per 100,000 in 1983 (Daly and Kelleher, 1987).

Public concern about the changing scale of the problem is reflected in two British Government consultation documents. The first, *The Health of the Nation*, was published in 1992 and aimed to reduce the overall suicide rate by at least 15 per cent by the year 2000 – from 11.1 per 100,000 in 1990 to no more than 9.4. (Secretary of State for Health, 1992). More recently, the New Labour administration tabled the Green Paper *Our Healthier Nation*, wherein they aim for a further reduction in 'the death rate from suicide and undetermined injury by at least a further sixth (17 per cent) by 2010, from a baseline at 1996'. Similar concerns are reflected in the Irish Government's Task Force on Suicide (Irish Government Publications Office, 1998).

Are suicide statistics valid?

Published statistics are believed to underestimate the true suicide rate in the population (Jobes et al., 1986). There are many explanations for underreporting. Some coroners may be unwilling to record a suicide verdict because of pressures from relatives of the deceased or the likelihood that the family would legally challenge their judgement. Regional and national variations in suicide rates do not necessarily reflect differences in actual suicide rates. The variations might be due partly to differing legal and ascertainment procedures (Barraclough, 1971). In England and Wales coroners must be convinced beyond reasonable doubt that:

- the event which caused the deceased's death must have been self-inflicted, self-enacted and self-administered; and
- that the intention of the deceased in initiating the fatal event must unequivocally have been to bring about his or her death (McCarthy and Walsh, 1975).

15

It is widely assumed that the criteria used in England and Wales are applied in Northern Ireland, although specific criteria are not laid down for the coroners. An inquest is held to help the coroner ascertain the cause of death, essentially to draw up a picture of the life circumstances of the deceased and to determine the relevant circumstances surrounding the death.

In Scotland, some deaths are classified as suicide by the Procurator Fiscal, others by the Registrar General's office. The classification of cause of death cannot be contested through the courts but the Crown Office states that there must be clear evidence that the deceased took his or her life. The Scottish procedure may make it easier to record a verdict of suicide. A death is recorded as suicide by a civil servant working in the government's Central Statistics Office.

Can we compare national suicide rates?

Comparative analysis of national suicide rates is of limited use if differing official rates are the product of substantial variations in recording practices. The usefulness of international comparisons of suicide rates may also be limited by the variable influences of religious and social attitudes on reporting practices (Douglas, 1967). Dublin coroners' records (1964–68) were examined to estimate the discrepancy between coroners' verdicts, the national suicide statistics compiled from those verdicts and the clinical assessment of probability of suicide by psychiatrists examining the same records (McCarthy and Walsh, 1975). It was concluded that while the Irish suicide rate is low it was not as low as the official statistics suggested and that the discrepancy between official and actual suicide rates was greater in Ireland than in the British Isles. The true rate of suicide in Ireland may be 15–20 per cent greater than that currently published (Kelleher, 1991). A recent study concluded that, contrary to the traditional view that social and religious pressures lead to greater underreporting in Ireland, the problem is greater in England and Wales than in Ireland (Kelleher et al., 1996).

The case of immigrant suicides

The analysis of suicide rates of immigrants has been used to show that there are genuinely different suicide rates for different countries. It is argued that if differences in national suicide rates are simply a reflection of divergent recording practices, there should not be significant differences between rates among immigrants. For example, a strong correlation can be observed between suicide rates for immigrants to the United States and rates of suicide in their respective countries of origin (Sainsbury and Barraclough, 1968). From a list of 11 countries Ireland was ranked tenth both for its national suicide rate and immigrant rate. During the late 1960s the World Health Organization (WHO) established a working group to investigate the validity of national suicide statistics. At that time the group concluded that the statistics were largely meaningless and served no useful purpose. Seven years later that position had changed: another working group concluded that the data were of great importance and recommended confidence in the use of official statistics from European countries for trend analysis (WHO; see Diekstra, 1993).

More recent research yields further support for the consistent differences in suicide rates across nations. Four large-scale studies, two conducted in Sweden (FerradaNoli, 1997; Johansson et al. 1997), and two in Australia (Burvill, 1998; Taylor et al., 1998), illustrate the extent of the 'immigrant effect'. In Sweden, FerradaNoli analysed more than 10,000 suicides and undetermined deaths, occurring during 1987–1991, and found immigrants to be significantly over-represented in the suicide statistics. This was particularly marked for immigrants from Denmark, Finland, Germany, Norway and Russia and, not surprisingly, these countries have correspondingly high national suicide rates (see Table 2.2 on p. 21). More worrying still is that the increased suicide rates among these immigrants were found to be higher than in their respective countries of origin (for the majority of nationalities), but the rank order was generally the same as that for their countries of origin. The Swedish study, carried out by Johansson and colleagues (Johansson et al., 1997), consisted of a study population of 6,725,274 and reported similar findings to that of FerradaNoli. For males who committed suicide in Sweden, the highest risk ratios, adjusted for age, were found among men born in Russia and Finland; furthermore, they concluded that being male, aged 45–54 or 75 and older, and born in Eastern Europe or Finland were significant risk factors for suicide.

Taylor et al. (1998) also investigated the variation of suicide, this time in New South Wales, Australia between 1985 and 1994, and recorded substantial socio-economic and migrant interactions. However, for the purposes of this review, it suffices to note that they found suicide risk to be lower in males from Southern Europe, the Middle East and Asia, whereas risk was higher in Northern and Eastern European males compared to the Australian-born suicides. The reliability of international suicide data for use in comparative epidemiological research was further supported in a retrospective cohort study: similar to studies in other countries, Burvill (1998) found that, when making comparisons of immigrants from England, Wales, Ireland and Continental Europe, there were significant correlations between immigrants' rates of suicide and those of their country of birth. Once again, the latter study confirms that national differences, despite divergent recording practices, exist and suggests underlying cultural and anthropological factors.

Catchment area analysis

Catchment area studies have been used to estimate national suicide rates. The process involves detailed analysis of suicides within a specific area and estimating the national rate by extrapolating from those data. For example, 410 post-mortem examinations in Galway, Ireland (in 1978) were studied by a pathologist and three psychiatrists (Clarke-Finnegan and Fahy, 1983). They agreed in 22 cases that death was by suicide. Extrapolating from these figures, they estimated a suicide rate for the Republic of Ireland that was three times greater (13.1 per 100,000 persons) than the officially reported rate. It was suggested that clinical rather than legal criteria should be used to classify suicide because clinical judgements are based on the balance of probabilities rather than the need for more or less unequivocal evidence. The suicide rate for Northern Ireland, estimated from three catchment areas, is 8.7 per 100,000 (O'Connor and Sheehy, 1997).

Simple aggregation of suicides and open verdicts (undetermined deaths) has been proposed as a method for obtaining more accurate estimates of suicidal deaths, although even this practice will yield underestimates (O'Donnell and Farmer, 1995). Some argue that these changes are unnecessary. A 1996 report on suicide in Ireland concluded that there was virtually no underestimation of the true suicide rate due to misclassification of suicides as undetermined deaths (Kelleher et al., 1996).

Arguments for treating as valid substantial increases in suicide rates can be illustrated through a case example of Ireland. Kelleher and Daly (1990) offer three kinds of evidence that marked changes in the suicide rates between 1970 and 1985 are valid. First, if the increase had been due to more accurate reporting, then, as the number of suicides increased, the incidence of open verdicts (undetermined deaths) should have diminished. The rate of open verdicts did not reduce significantly until after 1980. Second, changes in recording practices should have led to relatively uniform changes in suicide across the lifespan. In Ireland, as elsewhere, the suicide rate was traditionally highest among the elderly, especially elderly men, but the rate among Irish males under 35 years increased by over 300 per cent between 1970 and 1985. This could not be explained by changes in recording practices. Third, there was a very large increase of suicide in the cities of Dublin and Cork, whereas traditionally suicide rates had been highest in rural regions. This could not be attributed to constant changes in the way suicides were classified.

Several alternative explanations have been offered for the unusually high suicide rate among the Irish (Kelleher, 1991). First, traditional forms of social control have reduced in recent years, as reflected in a decline in marriage rates, increases in rates of illegitimacy and increases in crime. Second, there has been an increase in unemployment and, third, there has been a declining emphasis on religious and spiritual values that are thought to buffer against suicide. It is very difficult to test empirically the influences of these factors but it is known that there is a reasonably strong link between unemployment and suicide (Platt, 1984, see Chapter 4). If Kelleher is correct, the significant economic growth currently being experienced in Ireland should lead to a reduction in the suicide rates.

Can we compare national parasuicide rates?

There are no official, national statistics on parasuicide, nor are there stringent procedures to classify a self-injurious act as parasuicide. Therefore it is difficult to map temporal changes in terms of parasuicide rates and interpret these, confidently, with reference to variations in completed suicide rates. Thus the picture of parasuicide is unclear and incomplete: we can only estimate the incidence of suicidal behaviours that do not result in death. By way of illustration, as many as 120,000 cases of self-inflicted injury are admitted to general hospitals in England and Wales each year (Hawton and Fagg, 1992) and parasuicide is one of the most frequent causes for admission to Accident and Emergency departments (Schynder and Valach, 1997).

The WHO/EURO Multicentre on Parasuicide

In response to growing concerns, in 1985 the World Health Organization set up the WHO/EURO Multicentre on Parasuicide to tackle the alarming increases in suicidal behaviour that were being witnessed in most European countries. In the subsequent year, the WHO published the *Health for All by the Year 2000* document, in which they pledged that 'by the year 2000, the current rising trends in suicides and attempted suicides in the region should be reversed (WHO, 1986).

The study started in 1988 and had two broad aims:

- To monitor recent trends in the epidemiology of parasuicide, including the identification of risk factors (the monitoring study)
- To follow up parasuicide populations as a special high-risk group for further suicidal behaviour with a view to identifying the social and personal characteristics predictive of future suicidal behaviour (the repetition–prediction study) (Bille-Brahe et al., 1997).

This monitoring study aims to estimate the frequency of medically treated parasuicides and describe socio-demographic trends. Currently, there are 14 centres in 12 European countries participating in the study that includes five million people, covering the UK and Ireland. The repetition–prediction study aims to identify those first-time suicide attempters at risk from progressing on to a suicidal career. In some centres, the number of repeaters outnumbers the first-timers (Bille-Brahe and Jessen, 1994b). The study has five major aims:

1. To identify personal and social characteristics predictive of future suicidal behaviour (suicide and parasuicide).
2. To evaluate existing scales which are designed to predict suicidal behaviour.
3. To estimate the social, the psychological, and the economic burden of repeated parasuicide on the individual, on his/her social milieu and on society as a whole.
4. To assess the utilization of health and social services by parasuicides and the effectiveness of the treatments offered.
5. To compare differences in personal characteristics among parasuicides, and in the treatment of suicidal patients in different settings (from Bille-Brahe and Schmidtke, 1994).

Preliminary results from the repetition–prediction study were published recently (Bille-Brahe et al., 1997) but have been, on the whole, quite disappointing as detailed psychological correlates of suicidal behaviour have not been examined.

Who commits suicide: a male phenomenon?

In 1989, the WHO reported that only 39 of the 166 member states of the United Nations had submitted mortality statistics on suicide. There were a total of 208,349 suicides reported in one year. For all age groups suicide ranks among the top ten causes of death in these countries and among the top two causes of death among those aged 15 to 34 (Diekstra, 1993). Suicide is rare before age 14, increases during puberty and adolescence, reaches a peak at age 23 and remains constant until old age (Shaffer et al., 1988). In Western societies men are three times more likely to commit suicide than women. This ratio fluctuates across the lifespan but men are usually at greater risk. In England and Wales, suicide is four times as common in men as it is in women (Charlton et al., 1993).

Nevertheless, in certain age groups women make three times as many suicide attempts as men (Buda and Tsuang, 1990). It has not always been like this. In the early part of the 20th century the male–female ratio was fairly balanced, but this changed by the 1980s when men were 4.7 times more likely to kill themselves than women (Blumenthal, 1990). The largest gender differences are reported for Malta and the lowest for the Netherlands (see Table 2.2).

Table 2.2 Suicide rates in selected European countries (per 100,000 inhabitants)

Country	Males	Females	Total	M/F Ratio
Austria	33.6	13.3	24.95	2.7
Belgium	30.9	14.1	22.5	2.1
Bulgaria	24	9.5	16.75	2.5
Czechoslovakia	26.4	9.5	17.95	2.7
Denmark	36.1	19.9	28	1.8
Finland	44.6	11.7	28.15	3.8
France	31.7	12.5	22.1	2.5
F.R. of Germany (former)	24	10.8	17.9	2.3
Hungary	58.1	25.6	41.85	2.2
Iceland	23.9	4	13.95	5.9
Ireland	10.4	3.4	6.9	3.0
Italy	11.8	4.7	8.25	2.5
Luxembourg	28.6	8.9	18.75	3.2
Malta	4.7	0.6	2.65	7.8
Netherlands	13.7	8.4	11.05	1.6
Norway	23.5	7.7	15.6	3.0
Poland	20.5	4.3	12.4	4.7
Portugal	12.5	3.7	8.1	3.3
Spain	9.7	3.5	6.6	2.7
Sweden	26	10.9	18.45	2.3
Switzerland	32.4	12.9	22.65	2.5
UK	13	4.6	8.8	2.8
USSR (former)	30.3	9.3	19.8	3.2
Yugoslavia (former)	23.9	10.6	17.25	2.2

Source: Diekstra, 1993

In the UK and Ireland the increase in suicide among young men is particularly striking (O'Connor and Sheehy, 1997). Among 15–24-year-olds, suicide is second to road traffic accidents as the most common cause of death (Platt, 1986a). Between 1980 and 1992 the suicide rate for these men increased by 81 per cent in England and Wales (Hawton, 1994). In Northern Ireland the annual incidence of suicide among young men increased from 22.9 per cent (of all suicides) in 1981 to 42.1 per cent in 1992 (Register General for Northern Ireland, 1992). Young men were responsible for four times more suicides than their female peers. In England and Wales suicide rates in men aged 15 to 44 rose by over 30 per cent between 1980 and 1990 (Hawton et al., 1993). However, unofficial statistics suggest that in the late 1990s the suicide rate among young men is levelling off in England and Wales. Population shifts cannot account for these trends.

Who commits suicide? Is it better to be married?

Being single, widowed, divorced or separated are significant risk factors (Sainsbury, 1986). Married men are less likely to commit suicide than single men, interestingly, women who are single are not at greater risk. This may be because women are better providers of emotional support than men; and do not need the 'emotional crutch' that men seem to require. Although suicide among the elderly widowed has always made up a significant percentage of national suicides in many countries, suicides among young single people are increasing at an alarming rate.

Who commits suicide? The influence of social class

Suicide afflicts all social classes and the evidence on the relative vulnerability of different socioeconomic and occupational groups does not paint a consistent picture. Some argue that, as a rule, the higher the social class, whether assessed by income, occupation or educational attainment, the greater the risk; but a fall in social class also increases its prevalence (Sainsbury, 1986). Alternatively, it has been suggested that individuals at the extremes of social class, and therefore marginalized, are at increased risk (Shepherd and Barraclough, 1986). Thus, acute occupational stresses may be implicated in suicide among the very well off, whereas social and economic hardships are endured among the lower social classes. Suicide is more common in classes IV (semi-skilled) and V (manual workers), possibly because they are affected more dramatically by changes in economic circumstances (Williams and Pollock, 1993). Regardless of social class, some occupational groups, notably veterinarians, dentists and farmers, are particularly vulnerable. These differences may reflect the fact that these occupational groups are more likely to have access to a greater range of methods for completing suicide. Irrespective of occupational class, a productive work life is associated with reduced suicide and work-related problems are associated with increased suicide risk (Maris, 1991).

How do people kill themselves?

Traditionally, men use more violent methods to commit suicide than women. In the UK and Ireland men tend to choose hanging and women poisoning. In the USA men mostly use handguns whereas women poison themselves. The methods used reflect the availability of options, which in turn has implications for prevention. For example, in the United States there is a significant positive correlation between suicide by handgun and the incidence of firearm ownership (Gun Control Statute Strictness; Lester, 1989a). In a case control study

(Cummings et al., 1997), also in the US, there was a positive association between the legal purchase of handguns and the suicide rate.

The dramatic reduction in suicides in England and Wales, with the introduction of detoxified domestic gas, has been widely reported. In the 1950s poisoning by domestic gas accounted for over 50 per cent of suicides, but this decreased to less than 20 per cent in the 1970s and had disappeared by 1990. Subsequently the rate increased as alternative methods (e.g. carbon monoxide poisoning) were chosen (Williams and Pollock, 1993). Lester and colleagues have argued that suicidal people have a preferred method of killing themselves and that if access to the preferred method is restricted they are unlikely to seek alternative methods when actively suicidal (Lester and Murrell, 1980). Reducing access to more lethal methods, even if some change their preferred method, increases the likelihood of survival from a suicide attempt. Changes in access to means have been shown to be effective in one vulnerable population, farmers, in England and Wales. In 1989 the government introduced legislation about the purchase, registration and storage of firearms, effectively making it more difficult to own a firearm. Data on farming deaths by suicide between 1981 and 1993 reveal a substantial reduction in suicide by firearm, and overall suicide rates, in the three years following the introduction of the 1989 legislation (Hawton et al., 1998). The implications of these findings are discussed in chapter 9.

How is suicidal behaviour studied scientifically?

Everything described thus far is a result of work by researchers of differing types who employ scientific techniques to study self-injurious behaviour. What they have in common is that they espouse certain philosophical principles about the study of human behaviour and apply rigorous, systematic and analytic methodologies in the pursuit of knowledge and understanding. The review of the methods, outlined here, represents the dominant methods employed; this is not exhaustive and includes some techniques only in passing (e.g. case control studies).

Analysis of official statistics

The shortcomings of official suicide statistics were noted earlier in the chapter. Although a useful starting point for trend analysis, they should always be supplemented with other methods of investigation. Usually, official statistics save the researcher valuable time as they are compiled by a national agency. Trend analyses can also be calculated with little difficulty. Table 2.3 summarizes the advantages and disadvantages of each technique.

Table 2.3 Advantages and disadvantages of the different methods of investigation

Method of investigation	Advantages	Disadvantages
The analysis of official suicide statistics	Already compiled by national agency; relatively easy access; amenable to trend analysis, socio-demography	Classification procedures are flawed; difficult to compare across nations
Inquest papers and records	Relatively easy access; contain wide range of information: life history data, socio-demography, clinical, psychological data, GP and psychiatric reports	Not designed for scientific analysis; subject to bias; demand characteristics; retrospective biases
Longitudinal cohort analysis	Can be designed to suit experimental aims and objectives. Eliminates group differences	Time-consuming, expensive, loss of participants during study, suitable for detailed socio-demographic analysis
Suicide note analysis	Provides unique insight into cognitive, perceptual, affective factors; directly from suicidal person; idiographic	Limited use without life history data
Psychological autopsy	Useful for third-party analysis including: psychological, clinical, psychosocial factors	Time-consuming; tends to be expensive; retrospective analysis; subject to relations' own suicide schema
Interviews with para-suicides and high-risk groups	Information obtained directly from individual; cross-sectional, longitudinal, prospective; rich in information	Time-consuming; relatively expensive; veracity of self-report data questionable
Randomized controlled trial	Allows investigation of the effectiveness of specific treatment interventions; longitudinal; very productive	Expensive, time-consuming, loss of participants sometimes problematic

Coroners' inquest papers and records

Archival data sources are available in coroners' vaults across the country, but for the most part they are underutilized: they should be applied more widely in the study of suicidal behaviour. There are several reasons for the apparent reluctance to make more use of them. In the main, it seems that it is difficult to draw inferences from these sources because of the nature of the data. These data are not compiled with scientific analysis in mind, but to collate information pertinent to deciding on the cause of death. As a result, although inquest papers are of considerable importance to understanding the causes of suicide (Pearson, 1993), they are probably distorted by all sorts of biases, which can lead to vague conclusions. Demand characteristics, one group of biases, are a case in point. They can be defined as those characteristics of an experimental setting that lead a subject to a particular interpretation or decision. When someone behaves in a specific manner, as a result of a particular situation, this behaviour is a feature of demand characteristics. For instance, in an inquest process the gathering of information about cause of death may be biased because the coroner or the police think that death was by the deceased's own hand. Subsequently, this results in the biased accumulation of evidence to support this preconception.

Coroners' inquest papers often include a pathologist's report, depositions from family and friends, depositions from the GP and psychiatrists and other mental health professionals. With the exception of the pathologist's report, the other respondents may try to complete the deposition according to the reasons why they think the deceased committed suicide – not the actual reasons. If you are trying to explain the circumstances surrounding why a loved one committed suicide, it is impossible to be objective; we often extract reasons that we *think* explain the suicide from our own subjective knowledge and experiences (suicide schema). Therefore, analysis of the inquest papers is not completely accurate. That said, when the depositions are cross-examined and rated blindly and independently they can be extremely informative.

Longitudinal cohort analysis

Cohort analysis is used extensively in epidemiology. It involves identifying a group of people: for example, all those born in a particular catchment area in the same year and following them over time. The advantage of such analysis is that it is longitudinal, thereby reducing between-group differences and such studies can be devised to suit the specific aims and objectives of the study. On the negative side, cohort studies tend to be time-consuming, expensive and often suffer if participants cannot be found or drop out. Nevertheless, with all aspects considered, they are effective and particularly meaningful.

Understanding of the relationship between suicide, social deprivation and unemployment has benefited from such analysis. Glyn Lewis and Andy Sloggett devised the Office for National Statistics longitudinal study to examine death from suicide. This is a record-linkage study based on a sample of the population of England and Wales. They started at the time of the 1971 census (sampling around 1 per cent of the population) and recently reported on suicides up to the end of 1992. They have found that unemployment is associated with a twofold increase in the suicide rate and that social class and housing tenure are not related to suicide when unemployment is taken into account (Lewis and Sloggett, 1998). Other cohort studies carried out in Sweden have yielded invaluable insights into the validity of classifying deaths as suicide (Allebeck et al., 1991), as well as illuminating the role of psychiatric factors in the prediction of suicide (Allebeck and Allgulander, 1990).

Suicide note analysis

Over the years theorists have changed their minds about how insightful suicide notes are and how useful they are for understanding the suicidal mind. Often written minutes before death these notes are an obvious source of data, and sometimes it is the closest we get to the deceased. In the 1950s there was a surge of interest in these communications, followed by a backlash in the 1970s. Now most suicidologists hold the view that they are beneficial when studied in the context of life history.

It has also been argued that suicide note analysis provides limited data because only 18 to 30 per cent of all suicides leave notes. Some believe that note writers represent a special type of suicide that is qualitatively different from those who don't leave any. Research does not bear out this criticism: differences between note writers and non-note writers are rare and inconsistent (see Leenaars, 1988a). It could simply be that note writers are better correspondents or communicators than non-note writers (Stengel, 1964). The insights gained from suicide notes are described further in Chapter 6.

The psychological autopsy

Widely used, this technique involves interviews with healthcare professionals, family and friends of the deceased. From these interviews, the series of events and the circumstances surrounding the death can be pieced together. The psychological autopsy has been criticized as lacking objectivity, on the grounds that interviews are too personal and subjective. The loved ones are trying to come to terms with the suicide and apply their own 'suicide schema' to explain the death. These schemata are simply mental representations, attitudes and beliefs about why people, in general, commit suicide. Hence researchers may not be getting an accurate picture of the precipitating variables but rather an interpretation of the reasons why the bereaved think people kill themselves. The psychological autopsy should elucidate the specific risk factors associated with an individual case (idiographic approach), not the factors that the loved one suspects are associated with suicide in general (nomothetic approach). Case control techniques – that is, those where the researcher compares cases of suicide with non-suicide deaths, matched closely in time and socio-demography – are often found in psychological autopsy-type studies. They invite the researcher to make concrete distinctions between suicidal and non-suicidal deaths, and hence inform suicide prevention programmes.

Interviews with parasuicides and high-risk groups

Using this methodology is integral to the study of suicidal behaviour, for then it is possible to follow up people over time and investigate whether they self-injure, attempt or commit suicide. These subjects may be drawn from general hospital populations or any group known to be at elevated risk of suicide (e.g. depressives or schizophrenics). In this way, prediction models can be tested and more accurate profiles of suicidal behaviour developed. What characterizes a parasuicide, a self-injurer or a high-risk group is still not universally agreed, but it is hoped that the work of O'Carroll et al. (1998) will remedy this problem. Until then, comparative analyses remain hampered.

The timing of the interview is crucial, it is a constant trade-off: the longer the delay between episode and interview the more time for the parasuicides to re-evaluate and reconstruct their behaviour, but the more likely they are to be sober and compliant. Equally, the longer the delay the more likely they are to discharge themselves from hospital or to be feeling depressed after realizing the consequences of their actions. It is for the researcher to decide on what timing is most appropriate for the aims of the investigation.

Are suicide attempters telling the truth?

There is no easy means to determine the veracity of their stories. Research has shown that discourse is functional, it tends to be purposeful – to reach a certain end-point (Davies, 1997). This is particularly problematic when the interviewer is perceived to be part of the treatment process. For example, patients at risk of being sectioned, under the Mental Health Act, may be equivocal about 'the truth' – they do not want to be put in hospital. As a result, these data have to be treated with caution. The integration of various methods and analytic techniques enhances the validity and reliability of the data and extends our understanding of suicidal behaviour. Specifically, investigating parasuicides yields fruitful self-report data about the levels of hopelessness, depression, cognitive style and so on. These psychological characteristics of suicidal behaviour are elaborated on in Chapter 5.

Randomized controlled trials

The research designs thus far described are for the most part ideal for describing the suicidal phenomenon, and for informing suicide prevention and intervention programmes. However, randomized controlled trials (RCT) – stringently designed experimental studies – are required to determine whether treatment interventions are therapeutically effective. In their most basic form, patients are drawn from a target population and randomly allocated to the treatment group or the control group. After intervention, both groups are compared on a priori outcome measures; if the treatment is successful there ought to be a statistically significant difference between the groups, in the predicted direction. For example, there is a nationwide parasuicide treatment intervention study underway at the time of writing in the UK (Evans et al., 1999). High-risk parasuicide patients are randomly allocated to one of two experimental conditions: (1) a brief psychological intervention (manual-assisted cognitive-behaviour therapy; MACT) or (2) treatment as usual (TAU). After the intervention, the two groups are followed up six months later. In a recently published study, at follow-up, the MACT parasuicides showed a significant improvement in the outcome measure (levels of positive future thinking) (MacLeod et al., 1998). In short, RCT studies tend to be expensive and time-consuming; however, the outcomes can be extremely productive. They are described further, in terms of prevention, in Chapter 9.

Conclusion

Suicide is on the increase in most European countries and this has been matched by a concurrent increase in suicide-related research. We must come to a general consensus about what suicidal behaviour entails and how it is measured. The next three chapters describe the risk factors associated with suicidal behaviour, irrespective of definition or measurement.

Chapter review

- We must agree on a universal definition of suicidal behaviour.
- Suicidal behaviour is on the increase.
- In most countries, suicide is a male phenomenon, with considerable increases observed among young men.
- International variations in the suicide rate persist, irrespective of divergent reporting practices.
- There is a relationship between availability of method and national suicide rates.
- An integrated approach to the study of suicidal behaviour is required.

3

Suicidal Behaviour I: Clinical Factors

Almost all suicides have a diagnosable mental disorder, usually one of the affective disorders, although suicide risk is also high among schizophrenics and some personality disorders.

(Maris, 1991, p.7)

The traditional view of suicide is that it is the product of a profoundly disturbed mind. This position can be traced to the ideas of Esquirol (1838) and others who took the view that suicidal behaviour constituted prima facie evidence of underlying psychopathology. The converse view is that all mental illness is a form of suicide: any psychological disorder implicates a person in a process of increasing or decreasing the potential for taking his or her own life (Firestone and Seiden, 1992). The traditional position is founded on a considerable number of theoretical and empirical studies linking mental illness with suicide. Some of the earliest studies of clinical factors were conducted in Paris and based on interviews with the relatives of people who had killed themselves. Poor mental health was identified as an important factor in the majority of cases (Serin, 1926). Indeed so strong was the association between mental illness and suicide that by the 1930s many were concluding that clinical factors, rather than the sociological factors posited by Durkheim, were the most important in determining suicide outcome. This view received strong support from a number of investigations using different methodologies. Studies of coroner's notes for suicides in London indicated that at least half were suffering from a mental illness at the time they took their lives (Sainsbury, 1955). Similar findings emerged in American studies. Robins et al. (1959) collected details of 134 suicides in St. Louis and concluded that 94 were mentally ill, over half being specifically diagnosed with depressive illness or alcoholism. Dorpat and Ripley (1960) using a similar methodology concluded that all of their 108 suicides were suffering from a psychiatric disorder at the time of death. While these early studies illustrate the strong association between suicide and mental illness, it is important to bear in mind that the relationship is correlational, not causal. The vast majority of those with a mental illness do not kill themselves. While these early studies identified an important relationship between psychological well-being and suicide, it was clear that more detailed studies would be required to take into account factors of comorbidity as well as the severity and chronicity of any mental illness.

Those who attempt or complete suicide tend to share a number of clinical characteristics that set them apart from those who do not. These characteristics appear with remarkable regularity and are outlined in Table 3.1.

Table 3.1 Clinical characteristics of suicidal behaviour

Depression
Alcoholism
Substance abuse
Anti-social behaviour
Schizophrenia
Personality disorder
Suicidal ideation
Child abuse
Previous suicidal attempt

These suicidal risk factors are important to identify those individuals who may attempt suicide. The absence of these factors does not mean that people will not kill themselves. The suicidal are not a homogenous group – people kill themselves for a variety of complex motives and reasons.

Depression

It has been estimated that 15 per cent of depressed individuals will eventually take their own lives and that two-thirds of all suicides have a depressive illness (Maris, 1991). The lifetime risk of suicide in severe mood disorders has been estimated at 19 per cent (Goodwin and Jamison, 1990). Guze and Robins (1970) reviewed 17 follow-up studies of patients with affective disorders and concluded that 15 per cent of those with a primary diagnosis of depression die by their own hand – some 30 times the risk in the general population. Given that suicide rates are normally calculated per 100,000 of the population these estimates are extremely high. Most people in the general population who suffer from depression are thought not to receive adequate treatment and this is one of the reasons why its association with suicide is so strong (Lehtinen et al., 1990).

Depression is also a risk factor for parasuicide, but it seems that the presence of depressive symptoms, rather than a clinical diagnosis, is more predictive. This association is equally strong for adolescents and adults. An individual who is experiencing feelings of hopelessness, anger and irritation is at higher risk than someone who is clinically depressed and lethargic. Thus, it seems that people who are preoccupied with thoughts about suicide or attempt to kill themselves differ from those who commit suicide in the degree of depression they experience. Those who attempt suicide are more likely to express or experience anger, whereas those who complete suicide more often manifest apathy or there is no expression of anger prior to death (Macleod et al., 1992). Those who attempt suicide are also more angry, hostile and irritable than both non-suicidal psychiatric patients and people in the general population. In a study of 47 juvenile delinquents depression *per se* was a better predictor of suicide attempt than levels of hopelessness or a history of substance abuse (Harris and Lennings, 1993).

The contribution of depression to suicide risk increases when other associated psychosocial risk factors are present. Depression is a more important risk factor when, for example, someone is living alone or suffering from insomnia. Barraclough et al. (1974) reviewed a hundred cases of suicide in West Sussex and Portsmouth, UK. They obtained data on 130 items relating to the person's previous medical and psychiatric history, their physical and mental state at the time of death, and any treatment they were receiving at the time of death. Of the hundred suicides 93 were diagnosed as mentally ill and 70 per cent had depressive illness as a principal diagnosis. A depressive illness uncomplicated by other serious physical or mental disorder was found in 64 per cent of the sample.

Barraclough and Pallis (1975) compared 64 suicides with a diagnosis of depression to a sample of 318 people suffering from endogenous depression (a dated term which refers to depression resulting from 'internal' factors and implies that there are no precipitating events). Three factors distinguished those who had killed themselves: insomnia, impaired memory and self-neglect. Insomnia is often reported among suicidal people and is linked with the onset and persistence of suicidal thoughts. Barraclough and Pallis argue that impaired memory 'probably results from the influence of mood disorder upon cognitive function' (Barraclough, 1987). Self-neglect is probably a result of a combination of factors including low self-esteem, depression and isolation. A general predisposition to 'think of self-harm' and 'reduced social support' also characterize the suicidal.

The identification of these characteristics should aid in the identification and prevention of suicide outcomes among those suffering from depression. However, while numerous studies have reported an association between depression and suicide, few theorists have directly addressed how depressive illness mediates suicide risk. A Dutch study attempted to do so by exploring the association between national suicide rate, parasuicide rate (estimated from hospital in-patient data) and depressive mood disturbance (based on population sample survey data) between 1975 and 1986 (Diekstra, 1990). During that period the Netherlands experienced significant socio-economic problems which peaked in 1983. There was an association between depressive mood disturbance, suicide and parasuicide over this period, and the association was stronger for men than women. Diekstra posited that while women were more likely to communicate their 'unrest' (albeit through parasuicidal behaviour), men tended to turn to substance or alcohol abuse. Abuse of this kind can only accentuate underlying problems. In recent years, the average onset age of substance abuse has decreased, the number of men abusing substances has increased as has the number of young men committing suicide.

It is not clear whether different types of depression convey different suicide risks. Some studies showed that patients suffering from bipolar disorder (an affective disorder in which both manic and depressive episodes occur) have lower risk than those with unipolar disorder (Black et al., 1987); others found no difference (Weeke and Vaeth, 1986). Various components of depression have also been investigated in order to explain how suicide is mediated by depression. These have included low self-esteem, hopelessness, and lowered affect and motivation. Hopelessness seems to be one of the most important predisposing variables in depression and may even be a better predictor of suicide than depression itself. This may help explain why some people (the 'hopeless' depressed) go on to take their own lives and others (the 'hopeful' depressed) do not. We will return to this issue in Chapter 5.

When is a depressed person at most risk?

It is very difficult to monitor depressed people for extended periods of time. However, those suffering from depression tend to be at elevated risk at particular stages of an episode. Individuals in the early stages of a disorder are at particular risk and, as they learn to cope with what is happening to them, the incidence of suicide decreases with time (Hawton, 1987). There is some evidence to suggest that suicide is more likely when a person is coming out of a depressive illness rather than when in the midst of an episode (Maris, 1991). When the depression is 'lifting' the individual is both motivated to carry out the act and possesses the energy to attempt suicide. It is also thought that when depressed individuals have decided they are going to take their lives they experience a sense of resolution and calm; it may be that this calming effect also facilitates the final outcome. This calm is often reported by relatives and friends, who comment that their loved one seemed to be 'getting much better' in the days before death.

Depression and youth suicide

Some studies indicate that the most frequent psychiatric diagnosis among adolescent individuals who attempt or complete suicide is depression (Brent et al., 1993). Estimates of depression in adolescents are conservative, partly because the major diagnostic criteria (*Diagnostic and Statistical Manual of Mental Disorders*, DSM-IV and *International Statistical Classification of Diseases and Related Health Problems*, ICD-10) have been devised with older adults in mind, and because depressive illness in a young person is often misclassified. A European study of suicide among the young has shown that as many as 90 per cent were suffering from a mental disorder at the time of death (Runeson, 1989).

As part of the National Suicide Prevention Project in Finland extensive data were gathered on 1,397 suicide deaths. There were 53 adolescent deaths in this sample: 44 boys and nine girls. Depression was the most common psychiatric disorder with almost half of the boys and two-thirds of the girls suffering some form of this condition (Marttunen et al., 1991). The rising incidence of depression among adolescents has been attributed to sociological factors such as increased social problems (e.g. drug and alcohol abuse), extra pressure on adolescents to continue in education and so on. This analysis has prompted some to argue that the lifetime suicide risk among adolescents suffering from affective disorders is much greater than for the rest of the population because of the very high level of undiagnosed depression in this age group (Friedman et al., 1984). It is also thought that parents of adolescents frequently underreport psychiatric disorders in their children (Shaffer et al., 1994). For example, Poteet (1987) reviewed the suicide deaths of 87 adolescents in Shelby County, Tennessee, and estimated that one-third of the adolescents reported signs of withdrawal or depression. A significant percentage of adolescents who kill themselves are in their first depressive episode and tend to take their lives a short time after onset (Brent et al., 1993). These factors add to the difficulty of detecting and managing psychiatric problems in adolescents – both parents and professionals are unlikely to recognize the existence of critical precursors to suicide.

Depression and elderly suicide

Depression in the elderly is characterized by: mild to moderate severity, insomnia, weight loss, reduced activity and hypochondriasis

(Barraclough, 1971). Cattell (1988) carried out a study of 104 consecutive, elderly suicides in West London, documenting the relevant clinical and demographic details from coroner's inquest papers. More than three-quarters of this sample (79 per cent) exhibited depressive symptoms prior to death; 38 were men and 48 women. In the majority of cases the depressive illness had been present for at least six months. A later study reported a slightly lower incidence of depressive illness (61 per cent) in a study of the elderly population of Manchester who had committed suicide (Cattell and Jolley, 1995). However, the general contribution of depression to elderly suicides is highlighted by comparisons with the general population. It has been suggested that depression is evident in only 10 to 15 per cent of over 65s (Copeland et al., 1987).

Alcoholism

Alcoholism is also associated with increased suicide risk, but the nature of the relationship is not straightforward. It is a long-term risk factor, often the result of a 20-year history of abuse. It may be that in the short term alcoholism buffers against suicide, possibly due to changes in serotonin levels in the brain (Roy and Linnoila, 1986). In the long term, alcoholism interferes with interpersonal relationships and it is well known that reduced social support mediates suicide death (Murphy, 1986). However, it is not clear whether the reduced social support *per se*, or alcohol-induced cognitive and physiological changes, increase suicide risk.

The contribution of alcoholism to suicide in adolescents is substantial, second only to depression. As many as one in four adolescent suicide victims have a history of alcohol abuse (Marttunen et al., 1991). Alcoholism is more prevalent in men than women as is 'alcoholic' suicide (Kessel and Grossman, 1961). Diagnosing 'at risk' alcoholic individuals is problematic because they have a tendency to communicate suicidal intent frequently, and it is difficult to assess the seriousness of their resolve. 'Alcoholic suicides' differ in kind from 'depressed suicides'. The former often have hectic life-styles characterized by interpersonal conflict, individual crises and major interpersonal loss a short time before death (Black and Winokur, 1990).

There are very few prospective studies of alcoholism in suicide. In one, 88 alcoholics who went on to kill themselves were compared with 1,224 alcoholics who did not (Berglund, 1984). They were identified after admission to hospital between 1949 and 1960 and were followed until December 1980. Almost half (47 per cent) of the alcoholics committed suicide and were found to be more depressed on initial admission to hospital than those who did not kill themselves. Another longitudinal study indicated that a diagnosis of alcoholism at time of first admission to psychiatric hospital increased the risk of eventual suicide at least five-fold (Beck and Steer, 1989).

Substance abuse

The association between substance abuse and suicide is well established in both the adult and youth suicide literature (Harris and Barraclough, 1997). Some studies have found substance abuse to be the most frequent antecedent in suicide among younger people and a substantial body of evidence suggests that increased substance abuse may be a significant factor in explaining the alarming surge in young adult suicide (Bukstein et al., 1993). Moreover, substance abuse has featured prominently in the diagnoses of at least one-third of both adult and youth suicides (Marttunen et al., 1991). It is difficult to determine the impact substance abuse has on suicide as it is often comorbid with affective illness. The characteristics of substance abuse associated with suicide risk include recent heavy use, increased severity of abuse and associated aggressive behaviour. Substance abuse can also elevate suicide risk because it:

- disrupts important relationships and increases the likelihood of social isolation
- impairs judgement
- leads to acute and chronic mood changes which increase the probability of depression, suicidal ideation and hopelessness.

Substance abuse and contingent anti-social behaviour are also more important correlates of suicide in younger people who *attempt* suicide. Anti-social behaviours can be defined in many ways, ranging from hostility and anger to fire-setting or stealing. Some of the earliest studies of attempted suicide in adolescents and children identified aggressive feelings, preoccupation with fire-setting and homicidal behaviours as significant correlates (Teicher, 1970). A more recent study of 32 patients, admitted to the medical services after making a medically serious suicide attempt, found them to be: (1) more likely to have a diagnosis of substance-induced mood disorder, (2) less likely to have on-going psychiatric problems and (3) to meet the criteria for bipolar disorder or borderline personality disorder (Elliott et al., 1996).

Schizophrenia

The suicidal drive has long been described as 'the most serious of schizophrenic symptoms' (Bleuler, 1950, p.488); it has been estimated that 10 per cent of schizophrenics die by their own hand (Roy, 1982a). One of the earliest studies examined 500 people diagnosed with schizophrenia at the Johns Hopkins Hospital and found that, of the hundred who died over a 20-year follow-up period, 11 had taken their own lives (Rennie, 1939).

The traditional picture of suicide as predominantly a male problem is also reflected in the incidence of suicide among men with schizophrenia. It is rare for a woman with schizophrenia to commit suicide whereas 75 to 90 per cent of schizophrenics who kill themselves are men (Black and Winokur, 1990). A Canadian study found that of 16 suicides with a diagnosis of schizophrenia 13 were men. Significantly more men than women committed suicide during the first five years of diagnosis (Noreik, 1975). It also seems that schizophrenic men tend to be diagnosed at an earlier age and kill themselves after a shorter time than women (Harris and Barraclough, 1997). Moreover, 'schizophrenic suicides' have been found to be younger than both 'depressed suicides' (Langley and Bayatti, 1974) and non-schizophrenic patients (Virkkunen, 1984).

It is not clear whether different sub-types of schizophrenia carry different risks but schizophrenics who commit suicide are likely to be chronic and manifest numerous complications and remissions (Roy, 1982b). Persistent auditory hallucinations are also known to be a major contributory factor in suicide among schizophrenic patients especially when people feel they are being instructed to kill themselves (Roy, 1982b). Even when 'the voices' are not demanding suicide, they can be a persistent torment and impose an intolerable psychological burden thereby increasing the risk of suicide as a means of escape. It is difficult to disentangle the precipitating role of schizophrenia since depressive illness is often also present. Some studies have found that up to half of the schizophrenics who killed themselves were suffering from a depressive illness in the six months prior to death and nearly one third were taking antidepressants (Knights et al., 1979).

Most people with schizophrenia who kill themselves do so during the early years of the illness (Peuskens et al., 1997), and it could be argued that the effect may not be age-dependent but related more to the duration of the illness rather than the age of the person. This could be accounted for by the changing nature of the illness over time: depression may decline but other negative symptoms, including social isolation and reduced motivation, may increase in severity (Pfohl and Winokur, 1983). Suicide risk is particularly high shortly after hospital discharge with as many as 50 per cent killing themselves within three months of discharge (Roy, 1982a).

Personality disorder

The stereotypical view of suicide is that it is the product of a deranged mind. While this is a gross over-simplification, personality disorders are often associated with suicide. Borderline personality disorder and antisocial personality have been found in between 5 per cent and 10 per cent of completed suicides (Miles, 1977; Paris et al., 1987). Estimates of the increased risk vary, but it is widely believed that personality disorders increase the risk of suicide sevenfold (Harris and Barraclough, 1997). As many as one-third of youth suicides have been found to have associated borderline personality disorders and these conditions are also overrepresented both in clinical and general population samples of suicides (Runeson and Beskow, 1991). Surprisingly, we know relatively little about the way personality disorder actually increases suicide risk. Perhaps this is because personality disorders fit a stereotypical view of the suicidal mind: they appear to offer an intuitively obvious explanation and this has curtailed more detailed investigations. Individuals who tend to be at high risk are likely to be those who 'show marked liability of mood, aggressiveness, impulsivity and those who have become alienated from their peers, especially if this picture is complicated by alcohol or drug abuse' (Hawton, 1987). Borderline personality disorder is also an important characteristic of those who attempt suicide. Their actions are often impulsive and occur during periods of uncontrollable tension (Litman, 1994).

Comorbidity

There is a high incidence of comorbidity (the coexistence of disorders) among suicides and this may throw light on the mediating effects of psychiatric disorders. For example, Shafii et al. (1988) studied adolescent (aged 11–19) suicide in the USA, and found a high degree of comorbidity of mental disorders in the study sample (81 per cent) compared with their friends (29 per cent). Nine per cent of boys and 67 per cent of girls who kill themselves have been found to have two or more Axis I (Clinical Disorders) diagnoses and nearly a third have had both Axis I and Axis II (Personality Disorders) diagnoses (Marttuenen et al., 1991). Brent et al. (1993) carried out an impressive case control study on adolescent suicide over a four-year period in western Pennsylvania. They were interested not in the absolute importance of risk factors *per se* but in the role of comorbidity. Major depression was the single most significant risk factor, but substance abuse and conduct disorder were important correlates when they were comorbid with affective disorders. Substance abuse is most significant as a risk factor when it is present with affective disorder. Comorbidity of depression

in alcoholics is also a significant risk factor in adults (Mur
1992). However, a word of caution is required here. Many
comorbidity have not used a case control research desi
diminishing the ability to generalize the findings.

Alcoholism, personality disorder and schizophrenia are
ated with parasuicide. One study found adjustment disor
most common psychiatric diagnosis (41.7 per cent) for deliberate se
harm patients, followed by depression (19.6 per cent) and personality
disorder (12.3 per cent) (Shreiber and Johnson, 1986).

Suicidal ideation

Suicidal ideation is broadly defined as self-reported thoughts of
engaging in suicidal behaviour. It is by far the most common form of
self-harming behaviour. The issue of intention is central to the relationship between a suicidal thought and a suicidal act and there is
some debate as to whether a person is manifesting suicidal ideation
when they view death as a possible solution to their problems but
deny suicidal intent. Some take the view that intention is a key ingre-
dient in suicidal ideation, whereas others adopt a broader definition
based on the attitudes, values and general disposition of the person to
suicide (McAuliffe, 1998).

The incidence of suicidal ideations in adolescents is higher than
many suppose. In a large, nationally representative sample, 31 per cent
of 14-year-olds and 36 per cent of 16-year-olds reported having
thoughts of committing suicide (Windle et al., 1992). Some argue that
past suicidal ideation *with a plan* is at least as strongly associated with
completed suicide as a previous attempt (Brent et al., 1993). This also
applies to adult suicide: individuals presenting with ideations and a
plan should be treated as seriously as those with a history of previous
attempts.

Cognitive rigidity, cognitive constriction and other cognitive distortions are common in suicidal people. Cognitive rigidity is essentially a
form of 'tunnel vision'. The suicidal person is incapable of considering
alternatives and perceives the suicide attempt as the only way to deal
with the current situation. Not surprisingly therefore suicidal people
tend to be socially rigid: they are relatively inflexible and find it difficult to use a range of problem-solving strategies in their dealings with
others. Comparative studies suggest they are also significantly more
likely than psychosomatic patients and normal control groups to be
dichotomous in their thinking: they tend to polarize their thoughts
and examine complex problems in terms of excessively simple alternatives. This is reflected, for example, in the tendency to see just two
outcomes to the life problems they confront: to live or to die.

These ways of thinking have led some to conclude that suicidal behaviour is best understood not as a psychosis or neurosis, but as a 'more or less transient psychological constriction of affect and intellect' (Shneidman, 1985, 138). Ambivalence is, without doubt, one of the most common ways of thinking for suicidal individuals. Thus, relief at still being alive is often communicated by those who have made a serious attempt to kill themselves, while those who are preoccupied with thoughts of suicide frequently report a sense of fluctuating between 'wanting to die' and 'wishing to live' (O'Connor et al., 2000). As further evidence of this ambivalence one UK study found that 82 per cent of those who attempted suicide were found to have sought help from their doctor during the month preceding their attempt (Bancroft et al., 1977).

Communicating an intention

'People who talk about suicide will not kill themselves.' This is probably one of the most frequently cited myths. Early studies of the frequency with which prior warnings are reported offered estimates of between 55 per cent (Barraclough et al., 1974) and 83 per cent (Dorpat and Riley, 1960). Later studies have detected the presence of prodromal clues in 90 per cent of *retrospective* psychological autopsies (Shneidman, 1996). The frequency with which clues to suicide are detected in *prospective* studies is much reduced and therefore renders early detection more difficult. Thus, Shneidman (1996) argues for the development of professional skills in 'dissembling' as a key to identifying suicidal tendencies. We must dissemble the clues which are often abstruse, clouded and misleading.

Child abuse

The prevalence of child abuse among those who attempt and complete suicide has been ignored for many years. The limited number of studies to address this issue indicates that both abusers and the abused are at risk. Roberts and Hawton (1980) found that abusive or neglectful mothers made more suicide attempts than the general population. A later study replicated this and also found evidence of actual abuse or risk of abuse in 30 per cent of mothers who had attempted suicide. In Northern Ireland, Gilliland (1995) compared first-time adolescent suicide attempters with repeaters. A history of child sexual abuse was a significant common feature in those who repeatedly attempted to kill themselves by drug overdose, but not among first-timers. More recently, Law et al. (1998) found a link between the severity of sexual, physical and psychological abuse and subsequent deliberate self-harm in a sample of 257 females admitted to a general hospital in England after taking an overdose. Grand repeaters (those who overdosed five or more times) tended to have been more severely abused on all three types of abuse, to have been abused for longer, at a younger age and reabused in adulthood (Coll et al., 1998). We need urgently to acknowledge the extent of this problem, ensure that clinicians routinely inquire about abuse experiences and heighten our awareness of the subsequent difficulties experienced by this population.

Biology and suicide

There is evidence to support the notion that changes in brain function are associated with suicidal behaviour. Conflict is rife, however, because much of the evidence suggests a biological link between specific individual characteristics, like impulsivity, that are only indirectly related to suicidal behaviour. Most of the work has focused on serotonin (5HT) and noradrenaline (NA), agents found both in the central nervous system and peripherally. Depressives, and by implication some individuals who engage in suicidal behaviour, have been shown to have lower levels of a by-product (5–HIAA) of the neurotransmitter serotonin (a neurotransmitter is a substance that acts as a vehicle to communicate between nerve cells). Moreover, Traskman-Bendz et al. (1991) have reported more direct evidence with suicidal individuals: they found a double effect. Not only do these people have lower levels of serotonin and its metabolic by-products but they also possess higher levels of noradrenaline, together resulting in impulsive, aggressive behaviour. There is confusion over the actual role of transmitters in suicidal behaviour because lower levels of 5–HIAA have also been found in depressives, people diagnosed with personality disorder, schizophrenia and alcoholism as well as violent offenders (Winchel et al., 1990). These distinctions have yet to be clarified.

The relationship between first-time attempters and repeaters

An increasing number of people are embarking on 'suicidal careers' and the trend cannot be accounted for solely in terms of an increase in the level of mental illness or psychological problems in the general population. For example, Ireland has the fastest growing suicide rate among young men between the ages of 25 and 35, but there is no evidence to suggest that psychological and psychiatric problems are growing at a commensurate rate among men in the same age group in the general population.

The general increase in parasuicide has been matched by a similar growth in research aimed at identifying predictors of repetitive parasuicide; 15 to 25 per cent will repeat within three months of their first attempt (Appleby and Warner, 1993). Is it possible to predict those who are likely to repeat? Buglass and Horton (1974) have developed a six-factor scale designed to predict repetitive parasuicide. The factors are given in Table 3.2. The risk of repetition of parasuicide in the following year was 5 per cent if an individual had one (or none) of these factors and as much as 48 per cent if five or six were present.

Table 3.2 Predictors of repetitive parasuicide

Problem alcohol usage
A 'sociopathy' diagnosis
History of inpatient psychiatric treatment
History of outpatient treatment
Not living with relatives
Previous parasuicide

Source: adapted from Buglass and Horton, 1974

Buglass and Horton's scale has been used with two Italian samples but in these studies different clinical and social features discriminated between the repeaters and non-repeaters (Garzotto et al., 1976; Siani et al., 1979). This difference underlines both the heterogeneity of suicidal behaviour and subtle ways in which social and cultural factors may interact with and impinge on suicidal dispositions. A more recent study generated a more extensive list of predictive variables and these are summarized in Table 3.3. People who had three or fewer of the characteristics listed in Table 3.3 had about a 5 per cent repetition rate but those with eight or more had a repetition rate of 41.5 per cent.

It is important to remember that suicidal behaviour is a relatively rare behaviour and as such is difficult to predict, particularly over short-term periods of about a year. However, it is not particularly unusual in this respect: it is difficult to predict many behaviours in the short term. For example, in Kreitman and Foster's study (1991) nearly 60 per cent of those who had eight or more of the predictive factors did not repeat their efforts during the period studied.

Sub-categories of repeaters have also been identified and contributed to the earlier detection of at-risk individuals. Three types of repeaters have been described: (1) chronic repetition arising because of recurrent crises, (2) repetition during periods of stress and (3) one-off repetition in times of severe stress. Thus, despite the limitations of many measures designed to detect those at risk of suicide, they are

Table 3.3 Variables predictive of suicide attempts

• Previous parasuicide	
• Personality disorder	
• Alcohol consumption	more than 21 units per week in men
	more than 14 units per week in women
• History of psychiatric treatment	
• Unemployment	
• Social class (V)	
• Drug abuse	
• Criminal record	
• Violence (in past five years)	
• Aged between 25 and 54	
• Single/widowed/divorced	

Source: adapted from Kreitman and Foster, 1991

useful in risk assessment and lead to more detailed profiling of potential parasuicides (Kurz et al., 1987; Sakinofsky et al., 1990).

In general, prospective studies have found that those who repeatedly attempt suicide tend to:

• be divorced or separated;
• come from poorer socio-economic circumstances;
• plan the attempt more than one week in advance.

Retrospective studies show that repeaters are more likely to:

• report that they want to escape from an unbearable situation;
• have a diagnosis of personality disorder;
• be dependent on drugs and alcohol;
• be socially isolated;
• be more impulsive.

There also tend to be higher repetition rates among those not in paid employment and aged between 25 and 55 (Owens et al., 1994). The dissemination of information on the different types of parasuicide and their associated characteristics can assist in preventing future parasuicide, especially multiple repeat attempts.

Conclusion

The majority of people identified as at risk of suicide by virtue of clinical illness and other factors successfully negotiate many daily hassles. This suggests that it is the interaction between life events and the ways in which the person copes with them that is particularly important in determining the nature and severity of a suicide attempt. This interaction is outlined, in more detail, in Chapters 4 and 5, where we look at the relationship between clinical, social and psychological factors.

Chapter review

- Suicidal behaviour is repeatedly associated with a number of clinical characteristics including depression, alcoholism, substance abuse, anti-social behaviour, schizophrenia, personality disorder, suicidal ideation, child abuse and previous suicidal attempt.
- It is important to investigate how clinical factors interact with psychological and psychosocial risk factors.
- Investigating the clinical correlates of suicidal behaviour, in isolation, is not effective for prevention.
- Clinical disorders are characterized by associated (at risk) behaviours (e.g. insomnia and self-neglect) that predict suicidal behaviour (to some degree).
- The coexistence of clinical disorders (comorbidity) tends to increase suicidal risk.
- 'People who talk about suicide will not kill themselves' *is a myth.*
- Researchers and clinicians have had some success in predicting those who are likely to engage in repetitive parasuicide.

4
Suicidal Behaviour II: Social Factors

Suicide does not occur in a social vacuum. This basic premise was put forward over a century ago by Emile Durkheim in his seminal publication, *Suicide – A Study in Sociology* (Durkheim, 1897). His work is a good starting point as he was instrumental in promoting the scientific investigation of suicide and providing a social framework in which to study it. He examined the moral quagmire that is suicide with admirable objectivity and insight:

> *Following the publication of Durkheim's book, suicide came to be regarded by many as a social problem which was fundamentally a product of the nature of the relationship between the individual and society…the relative degree of disturbance of regulation; isolation and oppression of individuals in society were among the primary causes of the suicide rate.* (Hassan, 1998, p.7).

Durkheim's exploration broke from tradition in at least four distinct ways, as illustrated by Steve Taylor (1982). He was the first to develop a complete and logically consistent theory for suicide. Second, non-sociological explanations (e.g. race), according to Durkheim, were not sufficient reasons for suicide. Further, he argued that no single scientific method could be applied to suicidal behaviour but that its explanation required specialist rules and methods. Finally, Durkheim's work 'expressed an opposition to nominalistic reductionism', representing a 'break with the positivist approaches of competing works' (Taylor, 1982, p.7).

Durkheim's theory of suicide

Durkheim postulated that suicide was a result of society's influence and control over the individual and the resulting tensions of this rela-

45

tionship. Society constrains an individual in two ways through the processes of integration and regulation: by imposing certain social constraints and then by moderating our goals and desires. He proposed four types of suicide, each describing a unique interaction between the individual and society.

Egoistic suicide

Egoistic suicide occurs when an individual is marginalized, has poor social support and little connection with society. It is derived from the concept of integration; in this case the individual is not integrated sufficiently with society and is suffering from too much individualism. Suicide risk is inversely proportional to the degree of integration. For example, egoistic suicide may occur when an individual moves to a new area with no friends or family and experiences social isolation.

Altruistic suicide

Altruistic suicide is a result of society's expectations of the individual; it is the opposite of egoistic suicide and tends to occur when someone is overly integrated with society. Societal demands become too much for some people, they are unable to resist these demands and kill themselves as an act of conformity. For example, hara-kiri is a form of suicide in which society dictates that it is honourable to end one's life. Altruistic suicide is more often a characteristic of primitive societies but is still evident in modern society. One has only to think of the Waco massacre in 1993, when the disciples of the Branch Davidian cult killed themselves as a ritualistic obligation.

Anomic suicide

Anomic suicide is explained in terms of societal regulation. It is due to rapid social change and a sense of alienation that occurs, for example, when an individual is made redundant, or is in trouble with the law or when someone wins the lottery. Their social status changes, whereas during times of social and economic stability, the norms that regulate our behaviour remain stable. In this sense, we want and need stability; when we know how to act and behave, our behaviour is regulated socially and morally. However, in times of social or economic crises, the rules that regulated our previous behaviour are not appropriate; we are lacking regulation and this results in instability. This is why rises in suicide rates are found in times of economic boom as well as bust. We find ourselves in a state of moral deregulation, a state of anomie (the absence of usual social standards) which does not protect against suicide.

The characteristics of the crisis determine whether the anomie will be acute or chronic. A sudden drop in economic wealth (economic crash) gives rise to acute anomie but the precipitants of chronic anomie are more worrying as they can lead to steady increases in suicide over time. Durkheim was rather vague concerning such examples, but he suggested situations where society continually changes, placing individuals in competition with one another, thereby increasing the deregulation and risk from suicide.

Fatalistic suicide

Fatalistic suicide occurs when individuals have lost direction in their life and feel that they have no control over their own destiny. This is the opposite of anomie and occurs when people are regulated excessively, for example the suicide of slaves. Durkheim included fatalistic suicide in his theory more for the sake of completeness as it has little contemporary importance but is interesting historically.

Durkheim rooted the explanation of suicidal behaviour firmly within the domain of social science. However, the greatest shortcoming of his work was that at best it was nomothetic. From his predictions, we can identify the inhabitants of countries at risk but we have limited insights into the individual people who are likely to kill themselves. His theory was an attempt to explain suicide as a social phenomenon not as a collection of individual acts involving psychology. That said, he was not opposed to the discipline and attempted to define the broad psychological states that corresponded to his aetiological classifications: egoistic suicides show apathy and indifference whereas altruists are energetic, passionate and determined, and the anomies tend to be irritable and disgusted. These are interesting descriptors but not very useful for prevention. Nevertheless, since Durkheim, psychological and epidemiological research has identified more specific social correlates of suicidal behaviour; some are more often associated with completed suicide and others more often linked with parasuicide.

Social isolation and social support

People who are isolated socially tend to kill themselves more than those who are not. This is one of the reasons why people who live in rural areas are at increased risk from suicide. Social isolation is used frequently as a crude measure of social support, defined as interpersonal processes such as 'one person emotionally comforting another, helping to discuss problems, giving advice, providing material goods and services, and making another feel part of a social network' (Cohen and Wills, 1985). Inadequate social support is implicated in general psychopathology itself as well as in suicidality. The gradual movement away from important social relationships towards social isolation is seen as the first stage leading to suicidal feelings and a possible suicidal attempt (Jacobs, 1971; Teicher, 1970). In short, the lack of adequate social support networks increases the vulnerability for para-suicide.

Social support is thought to moderate and/or mediate other suicidal risk factors like stress and problem-solving ability. There are several socio-psychological aetiological models for suicidal behaviour. The two most prevalent of these are called the diathesis-stress models of 'problem-solving x stress' and 'social support x stress'. They are based on the diathesis-stress hypothesis which states that certain behaviour patterns (e.g. problem-solving ability) are the result of inherited predispositions and a stressful environment. These models predict that problem-solving ability or levels of social support become considerable risk factors only in the presence of stressors (Priester and Clum, 1993; Yang and Clum, 1994). This is an important distinction: for example, although we may have a predisposition for poor problem-solving we are only at risk when actually faced with stressful problem situations.

Cohen and Wills (1985) argue that good social support mechanisms aid our mental and physical health by buffering or through more direct effects. The buffering hypothesis states that in adverse situations social support helps maintain good general health but has little influence in normal circumstances. According to the direct-effects hypothesis this support is beneficial irrespective of circumstances. There is evidence for the buffering hypothesis. One study (Dalgard et al.,1995) followed 503 people over ten years and found that social support only protected against developing a mental disorder when exposed to negative life events.

Rural suicides

Being isolated socially is generally associated with smaller social networks and support systems. People who live in rural communities often do not have the resources and buffering mechanisms which are present in most urban societies (Gallagher and Sheehy, 1994). People living alone, irrespective of age, are more likely to commit suicide than those who are not living alone, but the elderly are at most risk. In one study, 50 per cent of elderly suicides were living alone at time of death compared to 20 per cent of the elderly population living in the area who did not kill themselves (Barraclough, 1971). However, the reasons why someone is living alone are important in determining the degree of risk: an elderly man living alone by choice is not necessarily at risk, whereas an elderly man living alone because of a recent bereavement may be so.

In Japan, elderly suicides in the period between 1979 and 1990 were reviewed by Watanabe et al. (1995). As in the Western world, they found a substantially higher rate of suicide in rural communities than in urban districts. Surprisingly, none of the rural suicides lived alone and almost two-thirds lived in a three-generation family. The rise in these rural suicides was explained in terms of changing social structures and values. Traditionally, in rural areas there is an extended family structure whereby people tend not to live alone but as part of large family networks. This has changed in recent years. There is now a propensity towards nuclear families, and a gradual and progressive dissolution of the traditional family structure that has engendered feelings of isolation and abandonment in the elders. These feelings of anomie predispose to suicide. There is a need for a systematic analysis of the social precipitants of suicide in this population.

Suicide and civil unrest

Durkheim also made predictions about the impact of civil unrest and wars on society: they have a restraining effect on robberies and fraud as well as on the suicide rate. The relationship between civil strife and suicide is illustrated by the case example of Northern Ireland. In the late 1960s to early 1970s, at the height of the 'Troubles' (between 1968 and 1972), Lyons (1972) and others reported that the suicide rate was unusually low. It was thought that the 'Troubles' created a great feeling of community and solidarity that led to enhanced social cohesion and buffered against suicide. This moderating effect is no longer strong in Northern Ireland (McCrea, 1996), and the profile of suicide there is now very similar to that found in the UK and the Republic of Ireland (O'Connor and Sheehy, 1997).

Suicide in prisons

Concerns about the incidence of suicide in prisons are motivated by several factors. First, people who kill themselves while incarcerated do so in environments where there is an extremely high degree of institutional surveillance and exceptional levels of control over individual behaviour. It is a matter of grave public concern that people should kill themselves under this level of state supervision and care.

Second, prison populations include unusually large concentrations of people characterized by well-established risk factors: younger, socially isolated, unemployed, men with a history of alcohol and substance abuse, family breakdown and behavioural problems. This has provoked concern about the level of additional risk imposed by imprisonment. As early as 1881 prison doctors observed that suicide appeared to occur at the start of the sentence, most frequently during the first week (Topp, 1979). However, calculating the level of additional risk imposed by incarceration, and the period at which the risk is greatest, is not straightforward. Normally, the rates for relatively rare events such as suicide are estimated for a period of a year per 100,000 in the population. However, prisons include very large numbers of people completing sentences of less than a year. In fact the average population figure for prisons per year is made up of many short stays by many times the number of prisoners. Thus, if the risk of suicide is greatest towards the start of a prison sentence, then the accumulated risk during a prison-year, shared among several prisoners on short sentences, will be greater than the risk for a person-year for one individual. This line of reasoning prompted the Home Office Working Group (UK) on Suicide Prevention (1986) to conclude that estimates of suicide rates based on the average daily prison population rate could be misleading. Instead estimates based on reception rates – the number of suicides per 100,000 receptions – are preferable because suicide risk is not constant over a period of incarceration and may be greatest towards the start of a sentence. However, there is a high annual turnover in most prison populations, reflecting the large number of short sentences served, and in any one year there will be a disproportionately large number of 'early' person-days in prison.

Taking these factors into account, a study of suicide in Brixton Prison, England, reported that the average duration in custody among suicides was *longer* than the average duration of custody among non-suicides (Philips, 1986). Other studies have drawn similar conclusions, indicating that the risk of suicide may appear relatively constant over a period of detention, or greatest during the earlier part, depending on the formula used (Burtch and Ericson, 1979). Prison management systems quite rightly focus their attention on the reception and early custody of prisoners. This is the period of greatest transition and stress, characterized by changes in family relationships, personal reactions to the custodial sentence, challenges posed in coping with prison life *per se* as well as pressures from other prisoners. However, it is unwise to presume that suicide risk diminishes thereafter and that extended periods of detention impose lesser threats to psychological well-being.

The complex issues that arise when calculating suicide risk among prison populations reflect a third cause for concern. The incidence of suicide varies quite considerably across different establishments. This may be due to variations in the concentration of prisoners at higher risk of suicide, or to variability in levels of awareness and management of suicide risk in prisons, or a combination of both. Identifying prisoners at risk of suicide is a complex task requiring two estimates. The first is an estimate of the likelihood of a person committing a particular action, such as injuring him or herself, and the second is an assessment of the possible consequences. How these assessments are made will be influenced by the management approach to individuals considered to be at risk. The factors implicated in risk management are summarized in Figure 4.1.

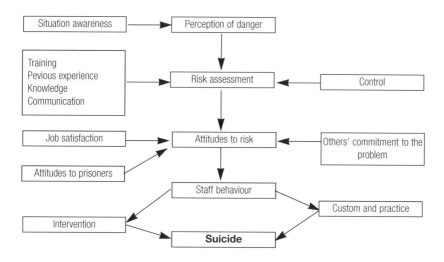

Figure 4.1 Factors affecting the identification and management of at-risk individuals

For a start, deciding on whether or not people are in danger of injuring or killing themselves is affected by an awareness of wider situational factors. Only by knowing what is usual or normal behaviour for a particular prisoner can staff detect anything anomalous. Thus, an assessment of the risk presented by a prisoner's behaviour is influenced by:

- the previous experience of staff in dealing with at-risk prisoners;
- their knowledge of risk factors;
- their communication of risk information;
- the belief and value they place in their own ability to control the situation.

Broader institutional factors concern:

- the job satisfaction of the officers;
- their attitudes towards prisoners;
- their commitment to reducing suicidal behaviour.

The actual behaviour of prison staff in terms of intervening, and local customs and practices concerning the appropriateness of different kinds of intervention, can also influence suicidal behaviour. Risk identification and management systems are profoundly influenced by attitudes towards inmates and beliefs as to why they may try to kill themselves. For example, any of the following beliefs could lead to different management practices on prison wings and corridors:

- prisoners who kill themselves are fundamentally different from those who injure themselves and are therefore impossible to manage effectively;
- inmates who attempt to kill themselves are guided by reasoned actions designed to bring about a change in a prison regime which has become intolerable;
- prisoners who injure themselves are 'malingerers': they plan to change a prison regime which is in fact quite tolerable but could be made easier;
- prisoners who try to kill themselves do so as a genuine expression of utter despair.

The principles of good management practice for dealing with suicide in prisons are in many respects those that underlie every approach to suicide prevention: awareness, education, understanding appropriate coping strategies and destigmatization of suicidal behaviour. These issues are examined in greater detail in Chapter 9.

Religion and suicide

According to Durkheim, Catholics and Protestants are at different risk from suicide. Traditionally Catholic countries have had lower suicide rates than Protestant countries. In places like Bavaria, Prussia and Switzerland, Catholic districts had consistently lower suicide rates than their Protestant counterparts. Durkheim argued that these differences could be explained in terms of the beliefs and rituals associated with each religion. The fabric of Catholicism is an established set of beliefs and rituals that keeps its followers closely bound. Protestantism, on the other hand, is much more individualized; the followers are more frequently 'alone with God' and therefore less protected from suicide.

The change in the practice of religious worship may also help explain the rise in suicide in many Western countries. Take Ireland: the number of people attending Mass, receiving communion and believing in the core religious concepts has declined in recent years. This reduction in outward religious practice, together with the change of emphasis away from the importance of the family, is thought partly to explain the increase of suicide in Ireland (Kelleher, 1998).

Some argue that church attendance and other social integrative aspects of religion, that were thought to buffer against suicide, are not as strongly associated with suicide as levels of religious belief and suicide tolerance. Neeleman and others found that, among females, higher suicide rates were associated with lower levels of religious belief and, to a lesser extent, religious attendance (Neeleman et al., 1997). This seems to be explained by the association between higher tolerance of suicide and higher suicide rates. They reported a somewhat different pattern for men; it suffices to say that the associations between religious variables and suicide rates are stronger for women than men. We need to look more closely at the relationship between suicidal behaviour and religious factors. For example, we are unclear still as to when religion becomes a protective factor or when it is a suicidal precipitant.

Are the unemployed more likely to kill themselves?

'While suicide occurs in all Census occupational categories and in all social classes, it does seem to be the case that work or productive life activities protect one against suicide' (Maris, 1991, p.11). Durkheim argued that work buffers against suicide, citing social processes by way of support. Essentially, an individual who belongs to an organized work force has a set of intrinsic social supports that help prevent suicide. Early research supported this association, finding that unemployed people were three times more likely to kill themselves compared to members of the general population (Sainsbury, 1955).

Intuitively, we can imagine a fairly strong causal relationship between suicide and unemployment (Lewis and Sloggett, 1998), but research has shown that this commonsense view is much too simplistic (Crombie, 1990a). Few of the early studies included appropriate control groups, nor did they consider unemployment rates of the general population. In fact it has proved extremely difficult to design a study to look properly at the interaction between unemployment and suicide. Nevertheless, a few studies, using control groups, reveal a significantly higher rate of unemployment among men who had committed suicide than among matched psychiatric controls (Roy, 1982). Roy looked at 90 psychiatric patients and found that 72 per cent were unemployed compared with only 43 per cent of the psychiatric sample. Robin and Freeman-Bawne (1968) also reported significantly higher rates of unemployment among men who kill themselves. We are not sure about the direction of this relationship; it may be that unemployment increases the risk of suicide or that people who are suicidal cannot hold down steady jobs and subsequently become unemployed. Stephen Platt and colleagues (1992) suggest that some individuals may be vulnerable both to unemployment and suicide.

Another pertinent question is: why do the majority of unemployed people *not* kill themselves? It is likely that there are types of people who habitually lose their jobs or are not motivated to get and keep a job. If this is the case, becoming unemployed may only be an epiphenomenon and not related directly to suicide. This is not excluding the role of reduced social networks and reduced self-esteem associated with unemployment that seem to have a more indirect relationship with suicide. More properly controlled studies are required to investigate the mediating role of unemployment.

Unemployment and attempted suicide

Unemployment is associated with attempted suicide as well as completed suicide. Platt and Kreitman (1984) followed up men in Edinburgh and reported a substantial association between male unemployment and the incidence of parasuicide. However, the relationship is extremely complex. Other studies have found that reductions in national rates of unemployment do not necessarily lead to a reduction of suicidal behaviour (see Platt, 1984 for a review). Social deprivation and poverty seem to mediate suicidal attempt and perhaps the distress caused by unemployment also increases vulnerability. Areas of high self-poisoning are characterized by overcrowding, poor education, high proportion of rented accommodation and high levels of emergency social services referrals (Kelleher et al., 1994).

Do life events trigger a suicide attempt?

A negative life event, like a relationship crisis, often triggers a suicide attempt. Additionally, people who are unable to deal with stressful life events in general and who have a pessimistic outlook on life are also at risk (Ovuga and Mugisha, 1990). Parasuicidal individuals usually have experienced more stressful life events than individuals in the general population. In one study a sample of 50 parasuicidal individuals had encountered twice as many major life events as people of the same age and educational background (De Vanna et al., 1990). In this respect, suicide attempters are also worse off than depressed individuals, who do not report as many stressful events (Paykel et al., 1975).

Notably, there is usually an increase in the frequency of negative events in the month before a suicide attempt (ibid., 1975). Suicidal children also experience more stressful life events before an attempt than those who are depressed or have a psychiatric diagnosis, and they differ in the type of stressful event. Depressed children often suffer peer rejections, whereas suicidal children are more likely to suffer social losses such as the loss of a loved one (Cohen-Sadler et al., 1982). Family conflict also places young people at greater risk from suicide and attempted suicide.

That's it, it's over! The role of interpersonal problems in suicidal behaviour

Divorce or separation from a partner and relationship problems in general, are often given as reasons for suicidal behaviour (Vlachos et al., 1994). Hostility, anger and conflict frequently characterize the interpersonal relationships of parasuicides (Nordentoft and Rubin, 1993; Williams and Pollock, 1993). Students often report relationship problems like the imminent termination of a relationship as a major precipitant of a parasuicidal act (Hawton et al., 1995; Platt, 1986b). Interestingly, Platt found no association between academic examination times and incidence of parasuicide, emphasizing further the role of social and psychological rather than academic factors in attempted suicide. This is contrary to the common myth portrayed in the popular media that academic pressures *cause* suicide or parasuicide. There is no evidence for any such link.

Parasuicidal individuals are less capable problem-solvers and it is unsurprising that they experience more interpersonal problems than matched controls (see Chapter 5). Schotte and Clum (1987) used the Means–End Problem-Solving test (MEPS; Platt et al., 1975) and found that parasuicides were impaired when solving social scenario tasks. Other studies show that parasuicides make more passive attempts to solve problems than people their age who do not attempt suicide (Linehan et al., 1987). Even young children who are suicidal or who have been involved in self-injury show deficits in problem-solving (Orbach et al., 1987). They are less skilled at generating alternative solutions to scenarios about life and death than non-suicidal comparisons. This helps to explain why interpersonal strife is so common in these groups.

In general, suicide attempters possess impaired social skills and poor peer relationships (Spirito et al.,1989). This was true of adolescent attempters who were hospitalized on a psychiatric ward; they exhibited fewer adequate peer relationships than a psychiatric control group (Stanley and Baxter, 1970). Among female adolescents, suicide attempters also have poor interpersonal problem-solving skills compared to psychiatrically disturbed non-attempters and non-disturbed attempters (Rotherman-Borus et al., 1990). In sum, poor interpersonal problem-solving is related to general psychopathology as well as depressive illness and suicidal behaviour.

Does bereavement increase the risk of suicide?

Bereavement often precedes suicide. Those who commit suicide are more likely to have lost a parent recently than people of their age in the normal population (Bunch, 1972). The risk increases in the four to five years after the bereavement, but is particularly high in the subsequent two years. Bereavement is thought to mediate suicide risk through social support mechanisms. Often, when someone close to us dies we lose a primary source of social support; the more dependent we were on the deceased the greater the degree to which bereavement increases the risk of suicide.

Is society to blame?

Some theorists (e.g. Naroll, 1969) argue that the well-being of a society can be measured using indices of certain behaviours such as suicide (Lester, 1998). For instance, high rates of suicide are symptoms of a sick society. Does this mean that countries with steeper suicide rates are 'less well' than those with lower suicide rates? Naroll (1969) thinks so.

Henry and Short (1954) give a more plausible explanation. They argue that when external conditions are bad we tend to blame our own turmoil and misery on these adverse conditions. As a result we do not become depressed but rather outwardly angry; consequently we are less likely to kill ourselves. Conversely, during good times, when our quality of life is enhanced we have nothing to blame our unhappiness on, so we subsequently become depressed and at heightened risk from suicide. Therefore, nations with a higher quality of life often experience higher rates of suicide. So, yes, in some ways society is possibly to blame.

Conclusion

Suicidal behaviour is a social phenomenon; this chapter has illustrated the intervening role of social factors on our well-being. Factors such as social support and unemployment are more precisely psychosocial. They are social variables that impact on our psyche to protect or predispose us to suicide. The next chapter explores the relationship between psychological and social factors in more detail.

Chapter review

- Durkheim described four types of suicide, each being the result of society's influence and control over the individual: egoistic suicide, altruistic suicide, anomic suicide and fatalistic suicide.
- People who are socially isolated are more likely to kill themselves than those who are not. Hence, those who live in rural communities are at an elevated suicidal risk.
- Suicide in prison is a major public concern; risk tends to be greatest during the early part of detention.
- The reduction in outward religious practice (e.g. attending Mass) and lower levels of religious belief are associated with higher levels of suicide.
- Work buffers against suicide.
- Suicidal people tend to have encountered more major life events than non-suicidal individuals.
- The risk of suicide increases in the years immediately following a bereavement.

5

Suicidal Behaviour III: Person Factors

At the beginning of life the common emotion is probably randomized general excitement. In the suicidal state it is a pervasive feeling of hopelessness–helplessness. (Shneidman, 1986)

This chapter describes the psychological risk factors within a broad theoretical framework that should help us understand better why people kill themselves. Consider Case 5.1

Case 5.1

RC was 41 years of age. He had a good job, it challenged him and he found it rewarding. He had seen his GP several times in the previous six months, presenting with sleep disturbance and loneliness. He had many friends and had an active social life. He had told friends that the only thing his life lacked was a partner – someone with whom he could share his life – the good and the bad times. He had first complained of loneliness shortly after his brother's wedding, which was eight months before he killed himself.

On the face of it, RC did not fit the traditional picture of suicide risk. He was employed, he had many friends and did not complain about stress and had not been clinically diagnosed with a mental illness. Loneliness and sleep disturbance were the only risk factors he exhibited. Is this sufficient reason to kill yourself? Most of us would say no. However, the case described thus far has only addressed the ostentatious signs of risk. Certainly, RC would not have been classified as being at risk according to the biomedical model of medicine, a risk factor prevalence approach adopted by many medical health professionals.

Let us assume that the suicide policy for RC's medical practice involves assessing the number of recognized risk factors exhibited by a patient. Say there are ten factors and that people who have more than seven of these are considered to be at high risk. If a patient, like RC, does not present with more than seven risk factors he may not be referred or followed up. This is not a criticism of the medical profession *per se*, but rather an inherent problem with suicide prediction and the model this profession espouses. It is extremely difficult to predict suicide because, thankfully, in statistical terms it is a rare event. That said, adopting a risk factor prevalence approach is less likely to identify someone at risk. This is particularly evident with young suicides, as they are less likely to fit into the traditional 'at risk' model.

The biomedical model

In its most conservative form, the biomedical model sees human beings as having a biological identity and argues that illness is caused by biological changes and excludes psychological factors. This approach does not recognize a link between mind and body – the mind and body act independently. Illness and health are seen as separate, not existing along a continuum. Exponents of this viewpoint believe that psychological factors do not cause illness; however, they concede that illness may have psychological consequences.

What does the biomedical model say about suicide?

The biomedical model predicts that suicide is caused by biological factors – to kill yourself you have to be mentally ill. About 10 per cent of those suffering from schizophrenia end their own lives (Roy, 1982a). The biomedical model explains this in terms of neurotransmitter imbalances. It is true that these biochemical imbalances predispose some schizophrenics to suicide but they cannot predict *which* schizophrenics will attempt suicide.

For example, patient A and patient B are both diagnosed as suffering from schizophrenia, they are similar ages and do not seem to differ in terms of the conventional risk factors. Within five years of diagnosis, Patient B has killed himself but Patient A has not, nor has he engaged in suicidal behaviour. The biomedical model cannot adequately explain why this is the case. Although proponents of the biopsychosocial model of health and illness (Engel, 1980) do not deny the biological basis of illness, they argue that it is the interaction between psychology, biology and the environment that determines health and illness.

The biomedical model versus the biopsychosocial model

The 20th century has seen the biomedical model challenged from several quarters. Theorists and practitioners reported cases of illness that had no obvious biological cause. Freud described 'hysterical paralysis', where there was no physical or physiological explanation for apparent limb paralysis, so he introduced the notion of psychosomatic medicine. The mind had a role to play in the explanation of the body and illness. In short, psychological correlates contribute to physical illness.

Other challenges have come from behavioural medicine and more recently from health and clinical psychology. Behavioural medicine, as the name suggests, sees a link between our behaviour, illness and health. The basic premise is that some behaviours are health-promoting and others are illness-promoting. Behavioural scientists argue that behavioural management programmes can be devised to enhance health and buffer against illness. Health psychologists have shown the positive effects of mind over matter. Their interventions have been shown to enhance the quality of life for many patient groups including cancer and coronary rehabilitation patients. Health psychology is well placed to tackle the problem of suicide.

Clinical psychology has been with us for much longer, growing in stature in recent decades. Clinical psychological assessment involves gathering information about the nature of a client's situation (the formulation) and subsequently testing hypotheses based on this analysis. The hypothesis 'testing' may include behavioural or cognitive techniques (or some combination of the two) whereby the clinician tests a specific intervention which will hopefully benefit the client – clinical psychologists cannot prescribe medication. Unfortunately, the medical profession does not draw upon this resource as often as it could. Both clinical and health psychology practitioners employ the biopsychosocial model of health and illness (see Figure 5.1).

In summary, the biopsychosocial model argues that the onset and treatment of illness is determined by the 'bio' (biological factors), the 'psyche' (psychological factors) and the 'social' (social factors). They do not act independently but in conjunction with each other. For more details of the biopsychosocial model of health and illness the reader is directed to Ogden (1996).

What does the biopsychosocial model say about suicide?

This model presents a multidimensional approach that sees suicide as the unfortunate end result of an amalgam of risk factor types. Consider Case 5.2.

LIVERPOOL JOHN MOORES UNIVERSITY

No. 379423

Self Collection of holds

Last 6 digits of barcode no. located on the bottom of your University card

Please issue the item at the self service machine before you leave this area.

ljmu.ac.uk   LIBRARY SERVICES

Figure 5.1 The biopsychosocial model of health and illness (adapted from Engel, 1980)

Case 5.2

The suicide of DF, a 22-year-old university student appears to have been impulsive. His mother had killed herself when he was less than one year old but other than this there doesn't seem to be anything further to note in his early life. The night before his death, together with his girlfriend and some friends, DF went to the cinema and then to a local pub. They didn't have much to drink, everyone seemed to be in high spirits and before going home, they made arrangements to meet up at the weekend – it was Wednesday. That night DF hanged himself.

Once again, in terms of risk factor prevalence DF would not have been described as 'at risk'. That he was a young male and had a history of familial suicide are the only factors associated with suicide risk. So how do we explain the loss of such a young life? Could such a needless death have been prevented? These are questions that were asked at the time. The truthful answer to the latter question is probably no, his death could not have been prevented.

More and more people like DF commit suicide without having acquired a psychiatric diagnosis (O'Connor et al., 1999b). These people are not abnormal or atypical. Suicide itself is not abnormal but, in many cases, a normal response to a truly dreadful situation. But impulsivity has a biological basis (a neurotransmitter imbalance). Does this mean that, like the biomedical explanation of schizophrenic suicides, these imbalances cause suicide? The answer is no. Psychologists give an alternative explanation: impulsivity does not cause suicide but it facilitates the actual suicide act. In this case, DF's impulsivity did not contribute to his probable feelings of psychological turmoil, the likely precursor to suicide. His suicide was caused by a variety of factors that encompass a wide spectrum of risk factor types. This genre of suicide illustrates that to get inside the suicidal mind requires more than medical diagnoses and biological bases.

The biopsychosocial model provides a more comprehensive explanation of suicide. That is not to say this approach can solve this growing personal, social and economic problem. However, it is more sensitive to risk assessment and better equipped to prevent suicide attempters graduating on to suicidal careers. The study of suicidal behaviour will benefit considerably from being placed squarely within the remit of health psychologists. Despite the advances within the discipline, clinical psychologists (O'Connor, 1999), all too often, still label suicidal behaviour as being 'abnormal'. Such categorization is not acceptable, nor is it helpful to the clinician or to the patient.

The suicidal mind

The psychological components of the suicidal mind can be divided broadly into intrapsychic and interpersonal risk factors. Intrapsychic factors are concerned with the cognitive characteristics that affect our outlook on our own situation, they may render us at risk from suicide. The interpersonal components are also cognitive in nature and interfere with our ability to develop and maintain interpersonal relationships. Bear in mind that there is an inevitable overlap between these components. Ten broad commonalities of the suicidal mind have been identified.

The commonalities of suicide

Edwin Shneidman is Emeritus Professor of Thanatology at the University of California, Los Angeles. He is also founder of the American Association for Suicidology and argues that to understand the suicidal mind we must understand ourselves. He believes that we have lost sight of the suicidal problem and he promotes a 'back to basics' approach. Social and medical science have failed, he argues, because 'they have lost sight of the plain language, the ordinary everyday words, the pain and frustrated psychological needs of the suicidal individual' (Shneidman, 1996). He has dedicated his life to the comprehension of the suicidal mind, the ultimate 'psychache' (Shneidman, 1996), the psychological pain which precipitates suicide. He proposes that irrespective of the individual circumstances, there are ten common features (commonalities) present in at least 95 per cent of all completed suicides (see Table 5.1).

These ten psychological characteristics are central to many of the contemporary theories of suicide. They help to explain the suicidal mind in human terms.

Table 5.1 Ten commonalities of suicide

1.	The common purpose of suicide is to seek a solution
2.	The common goal of suicide is cessation of consciousness
3.	The common stimulus of suicide is unbearable psychological pain
4.	The common stressor in suicide is frustrated psychological needs
5.	The common emotion in suicide is hopelessness–helplessness
6.	The common cognitive state in suicide is ambivalence
7.	The common perceptual state in suicide is constriction
8.	The common action in suicide is escape
9.	The common interpersonal act in suicide is communication of intention
10.	The common pattern in suicide is consistency of lifelong styles

Source: Shneidman (1996)

1. Suicide as a solution

We can all identify with many of these commonalities. All of us could find ourselves in a situation where suicide appears to be the solution to our psychache. This sentiment is expounded in the first commonality. Here we see suicide as the solution to our problems; it is the way out – the absolute exit. After a suicide, family and friends often comment that in the days before the death their loved one seemed to be happy, not troubled nor depressed. This is a common experience, the individual has decided upon suicide as the solution. Now he or she has no need to worry, or to be troubled, they have *solved* their problem, found a permanent respite to their (often) transient psychological pain.

2. Suicide as an end to consciousness

How intolerable must the pain be to drive someone to suicide? Consider Case 5.3.

Case 5.3

GL was suffering intolerably. He was not in physical pain, not that you could measure, but rather in a cauldron of psychological pain and despair. He had every reason to be depressed. In the last two and a half years he had been sacked from his job, his wife had divorced him and he had lost the closest members of his family in a car accident. To his mind, the entire world was against him. His friends had stopped visiting him. He had had enough; he overdosed.

In his suicide note he conveyed feelings of emotional intoxification. Every minute, every day he was tormented. Was he to blame for the deaths and the breakdown of his marriage? He said that he tried to move beyond these thoughts but could not. His consciousness was consumed by guilt and, as he thought, justifiable blame. He had wished he could have talked to someone, but that wasn't the way he was, he had never talked about his feelings or emotions. As a result, the only option he could see was to end his consciousness. Deaths like GL's are preventable. But to prevent them requires cultural change. Simply put, we must promote communication. Communication is a friend to life and an enemy to suicide.

3. Unbearable psychological pain

Shneidman describes unbearable psychological pain as the pain of feeling pain. It is the overarching emotion that probably permeates all suicides. The unbearable pain is the stimulus from which we want to escape. When we have a physical ailment, say a migraine, we take medication to reduce the pain. With psychological pain, there is no medicinal cure. The suicidal person 'administers' suicide to reduce the psychological pain. Psychological pain includes feelings of being boxed in, effectively incorporating all those emotions which torment us. Many of the commonalities described here contribute to this unbearable psychological pain.

4. Frustrated needs

We all have needs. Some theorists, like Maslow, would argue that all human motives are guided by conscious and unconscious needs. Freud and the early psychoanalysts viewed suicide as one possible and sometimes inevitable outcome of frustrated needs. Thwarted love can lead to frustration and is often a prominent contributor to suicidal behaviour in general and completed suicide specifically. We described psychosocial stressors in Chapter 4. In this context frustrated needs represent a psychological stressor. Like their psychosocial counterparts, cognitive and behavioural interventions can be devised to diffuse many of these psychological stressors.

5. Hopelessness–helplessness

Studies to investigate this commonality further (concerning hopelessness–helplessness) are prevalent. The hopelessness–helplessness theory made its debut in the 1960s, resulting from work carried out on animals. Seligman and colleagues exposed rats and other primates to inescapable shocks and investigated their ability to escape from future shocks (Seligman and Maier, 1967). They found that, after repeated exposure to inescapable situations, the rats became helpless and lethargic. The animals had become conditioned, they had learned that irrespective of their actions, the outcome would always be the same – inescapable. This learned non-contingency of responses became known as the learned helplessness paradigm. Using different methodology, it was later applied to human beings where a similar state was induced.

In short, the paradigm predicted that when we learn that there is no relationship between outcomes and our behaviour we are at risk from helplessness. Essentially, we realize that there is little we can do to remedy our own intolerable situation and we become depressed. However, this initial postulation was quite crude, so it was reformulated and called the hopelessness model of human depression. Hopelessness is thought to be the component of depression that is more closely associated with suicide. We are said to be hopeless when our thoughts are saturated with pessimistic thoughts for the future.

6. The cognitive state of ambivalence

Ambivalence is probably the most common cognition among suicidal people. We all experience ambivalence from time to time but suicidal ambivalence tends to be more frequent and affects a multitude of decisions. Suicidal people report extreme feelings of conflict, often simultaneously; they may alternate between love and hate as well as life and death. Consider the following excerpt from a suicide note:

Case 5.4

[name of intended recipient] *I spend my nights thinking to myself, do I love you or do I hate you? I cannot answer this question because it is probably both.*

This note was written by a 30-year-old woman who was separated from her husband. The ambivalence is evident; one minute she loves him, the next she hates him.

Some people believe that if we want to kill ourselves, we should be allowed to, without interference. An important consideration often overlooked in this debate is the psychological state of the suicidal individual. The majority of people who commit suicide experience intolerable psychological pain and ambivalence towards life and death. It may not be that they wanted to end their lives. Rather, they wanted to put an end to their *pain* and they saw suicide as the only way to do so. Many of those who make unsuccessful attempts are grateful that someone intervened and that they did not die. That said, the intervention itself does not reduce the psychological pain that mediated the episode, but it does communicate the intolerable situation faced by the individual. As a result, the precursors can be investigated, treated and hopefully remedied (we return to this issue in Chapter 9).

7. The perceptual state of constriction

Shneidman sees constriction as being solely perceptual. It is more useful however to consider constriction as having both cognitive and perceptual components. Constriction, whatever its medium, decreases our ability to seek or perceive alternatives. As a result, suicidal people tend to see suicide as the only solution to their suffering. They possess negative perceptual sets; this impoverishes their possibilities, thereby reducing the likelihood of finding multiple solutions to their predicament. This is one of the reasons why some people are more likely to see suicide as an option; they perceive the world through blinkers or tunnel vision – this is dichotomous thinking.

8. Suicide as escape

We all use escape as a means of avoiding unpleasant situations. In this commonality, Shneidman argues that suicide is the ultimate escape – the individual needs to escape from the unbearable pain. To this end, Baumeister (1990) put forward an escape theory of suicide whereby he sees suicide as escaping from painful self-awareness. The suicide act is seen as the final step in a series of causally related events:

Step 1   During stressful times we fall short of our expectations and standards.

Step 2   We attribute the blame (for this shortfall) internally; this leads to negative self-awareness.

Step 3   This negative self-awareness generates negative affect – depression.

Step 4   To escape this painful self-awareness and depression we engage in cognitive deconstruction. This helps compartmentalize our failings and attributions for failure.

Step 5   This cognitive deconstruction leads to disinhibition.

Step 6   Because we are disinhibited, we see suicide as more acceptable.

This is a cyclic process, every time we arrive at the final step we consider suicide as more acceptable and become more likely to kill ourselves. Baumeister's model, as outlined above, sees this process as being linear, moving from step 1 through to step 6, but it is probably more helpful to consider each step as being bi-directional. Moreover, this model is more of a heuristic tool, each step being the result of an interaction of events.

9. Communication of intention

Suicide is caused by unbearable psychological pain. Its goal is the termination of consciousness but it is also a form of communication. Using drastic means, we are communicating an unliveable interpersonal and intrapsychic crisis. Shneidman has compared suicide to a literary tragedy (like a Shakespeare play): with our mind as the stage, we act out a drama (trauma) inside our own heads.

The majority of suicides communicate their intention to die beforehand. In the days, weeks or months before someone commits suicide they emit clues. Sadly, often we do not recognize these clues until afterwards. This is not an indictment of the loved ones, but rather an unfortunate truism. It seems that the clues, the tell-tale signs only become clues and tell-tale signs after the suicide. That said, some people explicitly act out, or communicate their intention directly, e.g. ' I'm going to kill myself!'. We should never dismiss any such communication; unfortunately, the suicidal myth that people who talk about killing themselves will not still persists. That people communicate their intentions, verbally or through behaviour, demonstrates the intrinsically ambivalent nature of suicide.

10. Consistency of lifelong styles

The last commonality is not concerned with the precipitants of suicide but rather the nature of the suicide act. Shneidman believes that the characteristics of the suicide episode are usually in character – we are true to ourselves until the end. For example, if we are usually impatient (in life), we will not choose self-poisoning as the way out – it would take too long. We would be more likely to end our life through hanging or by firearm. This suggests that the choice of method of suicide is not necessarily related to the degree of intent (to die), but is more a measure of a person's own idiosyncrasies. Never dismiss a suicide attempt just because the individual has taken, say, only a handful of paracetamol. That attempt, in the eyes of the beholder, may have been as genuine and determined (and in character) as an overdose involving a hundred analgesics.

Behaviour immediately preceding the death also tends to be in character. Many suicides are preceded by a period of 'housekeeping' – getting one's life in order, paying bills, writing wills, visiting relatives and friends and so on. This seems confusing, even paradoxical. What is the point in bothering? Well, one explanation would be because that is how they have always conducted their affairs. Another explanation may be to reduce the financial heartache, to limit the suffering of loved ones, in some small way.

To recap, psychological factors mediate (and are mediated by) demographic, clinical, biological and psychosocial risk components. In terms of the biopsychosocial model, it is the interaction of risk factors and risk factor types that predicts suicide. For example, let us look at Case 5.5:

Case 5.5

PD killed himself because he was depressed (clinical factor) and feeling hopeless (psychological factor); he was depressed and hopeless because he was experiencing unbearable psychological pain (psychological factor); he was experiencing psychological pain because he could not cope with the break-up of a relationship (psychosocial factor); he could not cope with the break-up of a relationship because he only had limited coping strategies (psychological factor).

This description is quite basic but typical of many suicides. The components and sub-components could be analysed and meta-analysed, but what is important here is the understanding that suicide is not an isolated event but the climax to a series of interactions and, by implication, preventable.

What do suicidal people think about themselves, the future and their environment?

The cognitive triad

Aaron Beck (1976) describes the depressive components in terms of a cognitive triad: each represents a pattern of thinking regarding (1) one's self, (2) the future and (3) the environment. These are evident in the suicidal person and can form the basis for cognitive, behavioural and psychoanalytic therapies.

1. *The Self.* Depressed people tend to have negative thoughts about themselves, a negative self-image and perceive themselves as being worthless and inferior. They are more likely to blame themselves for these thoughts (make internal attributions), becoming trapped in a self-perpetuating system that promotes negativity.
2. *The Future.* 'This always happens to me, it will never end, what's next?' This is a typical statement made by a depressive. Depressed people believe that their current crises and unbearable psychological pain are always going to be present. They may become suicidal because they feel that there will be no end to their torment in the future. As a result some decide to end the pain themselves. It

is estimated that between 10 and 15 per cent of depressives kill themselves (see Maris, 1991).

3. *The Environment.* Depressed people feel that the world is against them, unreasonable demands have been placed on them and they interpret their experiences negatively. Despite feeling that these demands are unreasonable, depressives still feel that their inability to cope exemplifies their own inadequacies.

Life is not worth living: the role of hopelessness and future-directed thinking

Hopelessness is an important component in depression and even more so in suicidal behaviour. It has been shown to mediate the relationship between depression and suicidal behaviour among those who commit suicide. The Beck Hopelessness Scale (BHS; Beck et al., 1974), the most commonly used non-clinical measure of global hopelessness, is a 20-item true/false questionnaire that includes questions on topics such as 'My future seems dark to me' and 'I never get what I want so it's foolish to want anything'.

MacLeod et al. (1993) argued that hopelessness lacked 'conceptual clarity', for instance, it was not clear whether the presence of negative expectancies was functionally equivalent to the absence of positive expectancies. In addition, it was not clear to what time frame the hopelessness for the future referred.

By way of clarification, they developed a 'personal future fluency task'. Participants were required to think of events that they were looking forward to and not looking forward to across five future time periods – the next 24 hours, the next week, the next month, the next year and the next ten years. Three groups were tested: (1) a parasuicide group – recruited from a general hospital ward after acute self-poisoning, (2) a hospital controls group recruited from a general hospital ward after routine investigation and (3) a non-hospital control group, control subjects matched for age, gender and educational background. Standard verbal fluency was assessed and used to control for possible cognitive ability differences across the groups. No differences were found across the groups in the frequency of negative future thoughts, whereas the parasuicides were less able to think of future positive events in comparison to the other groups. This was evident both for the immediate and longer term future time frames. It seems that it is this inability to think of positive events rather than the presence of more negative thoughts that is associated with suicidal behaviour. This finding has since been replicated and seems to be present in parasuicides independent of depression (MacLeod et al., 1997).

Do you remember the time when? Memory bias among suicidal people

Depression is often characterized by difficulties in retrieving specific memories. This has been shown using a word-cueing paradigm, where participants are presented with one word and have to recall a specific memory associated with that word. Williams and colleagues (e.g. Williams and Broadbent, 1986) noted that parasuicide patients differed from controls in at least two respects. First, they took longer to recall positive memories about their lives and second, they tended to respond with overly general memories. Their memories were inclined to be summaries of experiences; they would recall a group (schema) of memories but not specific instances or occasions from this schema. These findings have been replicated and cannot be accounted for by intelligence differences or differences in cognitive performance (see Williams, 1996a).

When tackling suicidal behaviour, we need to address at least two components of depression: first, we need to moderate the memory bias, away from negative to positive memories. Mark Williams (1997) and others talk about this memory bias as a horse race. When we are cued by a word, there are several memories, positive and negative, competing to enter our awareness. If we think of the positive memories as white horses and the negative memories as black horses; with depressed people, the black horses are more likely to cross the finishing line first. In other words, a negative memory wins and our thoughts concentrate on that memory. It is not that the negative memories come to mind faster, but that the positive memories take longer. Hence, clinicians need to encourage the depressed person to activate more positive memories.

The finding that depressed and suicidal individuals are more likely to recall overly general memories has implications for problem-solving. We need to be able to switch between the specific and the general to be successful problem-solvers. It seems that it is too painful for a suicidal person to recall specific events and therefore they avoid doing so. They do not process the emotional content of these memories. In terms of schema theory, suicidal individuals identify the schema (general memory) but do not search beyond this to retrieve a specific event.

Memory biases and interpersonal problem-solving ability

These memory biases explain, to some degree, why suicidal people exhibit impaired interpersonal problem-solving skills. Williams describes this bias towards over generalization as 'mnemonic interlock' (Williams, 1997). The patients are caught between levels of memory, they are able to access the general memories but are unable to generate specific autobiographical memories from these. They are locked in an intermediate stage of processing which is analogous to finding your own house (general memories) but not being able to get inside (specific memories).

To assess problem-solving ability, most researchers employ the Means–End Problem-Solving procedure (MEPS; Platt et al., 1975). This is 'a measure of the ability to conceptualize, in interpersonal situations, appropriate and effective means to reach a specified goal'. Participants are presented with different social scenarios, each describing an initial problem and a desired outcome. Their task is to generate the means to obtain this outcome. Problem-solving ability is measured in terms of the numbers of means generated, whether they were relevant or irrelevant solutions, and the number of obstacles they thought they would encounter. Suicidal people consistently perform less well than matched comparisons. They generate fewer solutions and less relevant solutions with more obstacles.

Are there any other solutions? The role of cognitive rigidity

Schotte and Clum (1982, 1987) proposed, in the diathesis–stress model, that cognitive rigidity mediated between negative life events and suicidal behaviour. They argued that those individuals exhibiting cognitive rigidity or dichotomous thinking quickly became overwhelmed by life stress, which places them at risk from suicidal behaviour. They later added hopelessness and interpersonal problem-solving ability to this model. The presence of hopelessness, cognitive rigidity and life stress impairs problem-solving ability and places us at risk from suicidal behaviour. Suicidal ideators tend to be less active in their problem-solving and focus on negative outcomes. The relationship between these is particularly complex and not well understood.

Why does it always happen to me? The role of attributions

Chris Peterson, Lynn Abramson and colleagues devised the Attributional Style Questionnaire (ASQ; Peterson et al., 1982) and have shown that depressed and suicidal people exhibit a depressogenic (negative) attributional style. This is measured along three dimensions: internal–external, stable–unstable, global–specific. Respondents are told to imagine themselves vividly in twelve situations (six are positive and six are negative; six are interpersonal and six are achievement related) and write down what they consider to be the situation's major cause. Depressed people tend to attribute negative events to internal, stable and global causes and successes to external and unstable causes. They blame themselves for the event (internal) they think that the causes will always be present (stable) and will interfere with all aspects of their life in the future (global). Once started, this negative cognitive style is self-perpetuating and difficult to modify, representing another cognitive interlock.

Negative cognitive style has been incorporated into the diathesis-stress model and has been shown to be a stress-mediated depressogenic vulnerability factor. The combination of stress and negative attributional style can lead to hopelessness which, in turn, can lead to suicidal behaviour. More specifically, negative attributional style for interpersonal events (not achievement events) and the presence of interpersonal life stresses are related to self-reported suicidal ideation. The ASQ has recently been upgraded to the Cognitive Style Questionnaire (CSQ) and includes items to measure consequences and the self-worth implications of the events (Abramson et al., 1998). Controllability, the degree to which people are in control of their circumstances, has also been shown to be a risk factor. In some cases, when controllability is low suicide risk is high.

It's just not good enough! The role of perfectionism

Perfectionism is another variable that has received considerable interest recently as a predictor of suicidal behaviours. Perfectionism is generally characterized by individuals who set unrealistically high goals and standards and they tend to be overly self-critical. It has been implicated in numerous clinical disorders including eating disorders, alcoholism, obsessive compulsive disorder and personality disorders (see Pacht, 1984).

The seriousness of this psychological construct has long been recognized but much of the empirical work was halted because there was no consensus as to the nature and definition of perfectionism. That perfectionists set excessively high standards for themselves is, in itself, not enough to distinguish normal perfectionists from neurotic perfectionists (see Hamachek, 1978). Normal perfectionists set high standards but understand that sometimes it is not possible to meet these standards, whereas the neurotic perfectionists are more excessive, almost believing that perfection cannot be attained and they do not allow for mistakes.

There are several dimensions of perfectionism that appear to predict psychopathology:

- level of concern over mistakes;
- evaluation of quality of own performance;
- value of parental (significant other) evaluation and expectations;
- emphasis on order and organization.

Psychopathological perfectionists are overly concerned with the most minor of mistakes. They also doubt their own ability and tend to perceive a task as a failure if it includes even a hint of a mistake. This may be linked to parental rearing styles, whereby parental love was conditional on performance. One outcome is that perfectionists are driven by the fear of failure rather than the desire for success. This makes them choose suicide rather than failure. Perfectionists tend to place too much emphasis on orderliness and this is evident in their day-to-day activities.

Case 5.6 describes the perfectionistic tendencies of a woman, aged 23 years, who killed herself. This description is paraphrased from coroner's inquest papers.

Case 5.6

Her brother remarked: *CB was always commenting on the importance of carrying things out correctly. It didn't matter whether she was washing clothes or writing a work report. She always said she was a perfectionist. CB had never failed in anything but still was so concerned with what other people thought of her.*

Friend of deceased: *Sometimes I used to wonder why she was so driven, why she placed such demands on herself. I know now, even though she was 23 years of age, she thought it was the only way to impress her mother.*

These descriptions illustrate (1) the perfectionistic tendencies of CB and (2) the (apparent) demands placed on her by significant others. When considering the components of perfectionism in suicidal behaviour, the perfection we demand of ourselves (self-oriented perfection) and the perfection demands of significant others (socially prescribed perfection) are of importance. These components have been incorporated into the Multidimensional Perfectionism Scale (Hewitt and Flett, 1991).

Hewitt and colleagues have shown that self and socially prescribed perfectionism are associated with suicidal ideation, even when depression and hopelessness are taken into account. They posit several explanations; perfectionists constantly fail (by their own standards); these failures impact on their self-esteem, further exacerbating the failure. A second explanation is a form of social hopelessness, defined as the inability to control other people's expectations. Perfectionists believe that they have not lived up to other people's expectations of them, they cannot control what others think of them and this pains them greatly.

At some stage we all encounter the traditional suicide risk factors but most of us do not kill ourselves. So, then, what differentiates us from those who do try to kill themselves? We differ, at least, in terms of psychological risk and protective factors. According to the model outlined here (see Figure 5.2), even when bombarded by traditional risk factors people remain at low risk if, for example, they are good problem-solvers, have reasons for living, have good communication skills and so on. These are the factors that buffer against hopelessness, depression and ultimately suicide. However, they become more at risk when they possess poor problem-solving skills, have few positive thoughts for the future, a negative cognitive style and reduced social supports. Much more work is yet to be done to further the comprehension of these distinctions. Nevertheless, this model provides a useful framework on which to base future research.

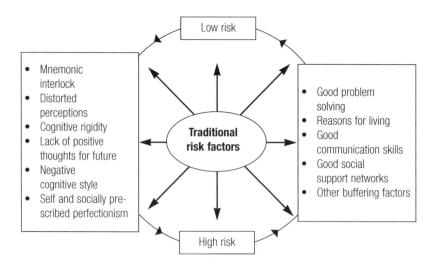

Figure 5.2 A psychological model of suicidal behaviour

Conclusion

In recent years, social scientists have made important advances in understanding the psychology of the suicidal mind. The acceptance of the biopsychosocial model has led the way for more integrative models of suicidal behaviour (e.g. the diathesis-stress model) which are more sensitive to suicide risk assessment. What is important is the understanding of the process of risk. Devising a checklist of suicide risk factors is not sufficient to identify the individuals who are at risk. We need to look at how these variables affect someone's individual psyche to distort their perceptions and cognitions. The next chapter considers the suicidal mind directly by analysing suicide letters – the closest we can get to the suicidal mind.

Chapter review

- The biomedical and biopsychosocial models of health and illness offer differing explanations for suicidal behaviour.
- Psychologists support the biopsychosocial model, which argues that illness is determined by the interaction of biological, psychological and social factors.
- Ten common features (commonalities) of suicidal behaviour are described, including unbearable psychological pain, frustration, hopelessness and cognitive constriction.
- The escape theory of suicide (Baumeister, 1990) sees suicide as an escape from painful self-awareness.
- Suicidal thoughts are characterized by a negative preoccupation about: one's self, the future and the environment (Beck's cognitive triad).
- Hopelessness is commonly associated with suicidal behaviour. In particular, parasuicides are less able to think about future positive events in comparison to non-parasuicides. They also have difficulty in retrieving specific memories, take longer to recall positive experiences and are less effective problem-solvers.
- Depressed and suicidal people exhibit a depressogenic attributional style.
- Suicidal individuals tend to possess perfectionistic tendencies.
- Checklist approaches to risk assessment must be supplemented by determining how the traditional risk factors affect our cognitions and perceptions.

6

Suicide Communication I: Suicide Letters

Suicide notes are the ultrapersonal documents. They are the unsolicited productions of the suicidal person, usually written minutes before the suicidal death. They are an invaluable starting point for comprehending the suicidal act and for understanding the special features of the people who actually commit suicide and what they share in common with the rest of us who have only been drawn to imagine it. (Leenaars, 1988a, p. 34).

Suicide notes, diaries and letters can provide valuable insights into the thoughts and feelings of the suicidal person. The bereaved often expect these documents to contain the 'truth' – the reason why suicide was visited upon them – although in many instances the suicide note does not provide the answers they hoped for. Suicide notes are enormously varied. Some hold directions to where the deceased may be found: 'You will find me in the river.' Others are akin to wills: 'I leave everything to my little brother.' Still others are aggressive and provocative: 'I hope this makes you happy now!'

Whereas Durkheim and neo-Durkheimian theorists provided a broad sociological framework for understanding suicide, analysts of suicide notes have provided important insights into why specific individuals kill themselves.

Brief history of suicide note analysis

Suicide notes *'contain special revelations of the human mind and [that] there is much one can learn from them'*. (Shneidman, 1980, p. 12)

Over the last 50 years Edwin Shneidman has changed his assessment of the usefulness of suicide note analysis. In the 1950s he believed that these personal documents were the best way to study psychological components of the suicidal mind, terming this his 'thesis' (Shneidman and Farberow, 1957). By the 1970s he had turned 180 degrees and argued that the psychological insights provided by these documents were only useful for understanding why the author of a particular suicide note had acted as they did, not why people in general commit suicide. He took the view that the suicidal mind is so constricted that anything communicated in a note could not be meaningfully interpreted; this was his 'antithesis' (Shneidman, 1973). More recently he has adopted a pragmatic perspective which he terms 'synthesis': analysis of suicide notes, framed within a wider psychosocial context, can inform our understanding of suicidal despair. 'Many suicide notes, when taken in the context of life history of that individual who wrote the note, [can] throw enormous light on the life, just as the life [can] help illuminate many aspects of the note' (Shneidman, 1988: 10).

Limitations of suicide notes

Between 15 and 30 per cent of those who kill themselves leave notes. This raises the possibility that note writers may be quite different from the majority of those who commit suicide but fail to leave a final communication. Several studies have looked at possible differences between note writers and non-note writers, but few differences have been found. The demographic profile of these two groups is very similar (Leenaars, 1989; Shneidman, 1981; Shneidman and Farberow, 1960; Tuckman et al., 1959). Leenaars reviewed the suicide notes written by North American men and women for the presence of 50 psychological themes and reported no sex differences (Leenaars, 1988a). Stengel (1964) pointed out that note writers may simply be better correspondents than non-note writers and implied that it may be valid to generalize the findings from suicide note analysis to all instances of suicide.

Others argue that there is no place for suicide note analysis in science because studying individuals, in itself, is unscientific. Leenaars (1988a, b) and Shneidman (1985) strongly disagree. The problems associated with the analysis of personal documents have long been recognized (Allport, 1942) but we can learn much about the individual from such documents, advance both idiographic (individual) and nomothetic (group) standpoints and further the aims of science in understanding, predicting and controlling suicidal behaviour. Shneidman (1980) has offered a good yardstick: provided theorists analyse the notes in the context of the deceased's life and experiences they will be useful tools in the explanation of suicidal behaviour.

How may suicide notes be analysed?

Suicide note analysis can be organized into three types. The first is descriptive analysis, principally concerned with describing demo-graphic, cognitive, situational and emotional characteristics of the deceased. The second addresses differences between genuine and sim-ulated suicide notes. Simulated suicide notes are authored by people who write 'as if' they were about to commit suicide. Any differences observed between the notes written by these two groups are attributed to differences in suicidality. The third type of analysis uses a structured framework, the Thematic Guide to Suicide Prediction (TGSP; Leenaars, 1992, 1996), to categorize suicide notes according to a number of intrapsychic and interpersonal variables.

What do suicide notes tell us about suicide?

One of the earliest systematic descriptions of suicide notes was offered by Freud (Freud, 1905/1974) who was concerned that these docu-ments were largely ignored in suicide research and argued for the psy-chodynamic significance of their content. More recently, Leenaars (1988a) has published an extensive review of the history of suicide note analysis and concluded that published studies could be grouped into five classes:

- the situation of the person who committed suicide;
- the relationship between the deceased and someone else;
- the emotional state of the deceased;
- the cognitive state of the deceased;
- demographic details.

Situational factors

Suicide notes are communications that characteristically convey a pro-found sense of psychological loss and pain (Shneidman, 1980; Bjerg, 1967; Wagner, 1960). The note is often written in a form intended to elicit a response or a solution from the reader but received too late to achieve this goal. Thus, the note often conveys a sense of someone who has chosen a permanent solution to a temporary problem.

Relationship factors

Relationships between the writer and significant others are frequently cited in suicide notes. The writer sometimes tries to communicate feel-ings of rejection (Leenaars, 1988a), despair for the paltry nature of their interpersonal attachments (Leenaars and Balance, 1984a) and height-ened dependency (Darbonne, 1969).

Emotional factors

The emotional state of the writer often fills an important part of the suicide note, and feelings of bitterness, animosity and open hostility to others are often recorded (Leenaars and Balance, 1984b). More than any other psychological state, suicidal people report an inability to develop or maintain meaningful or lasting relationships. Thus, within a psychodynamic framework suicide is seen as 'murder in the 180th degree' (Shneidman, 1980), aggression directed inward. Other emotions are evident, including hopelessness, helplessness, frustration, and despair (Shneidman, 1985). Feelings of ambivalence combined with emotional conflicts are also prevalent, for example the co-existence of both love and hate for a particular person (Ogilvie et al., 1969).

Cognitive factors

One could reasonably expect evidence of the cognitive state of the suicidal person to be manifest in their suicide note and analysis has revealed striking distortions in thinking indicative of cognitive constriction (Shneidman, 1985). The writers will often describe a situation that to them appears completely rational but which conveys to a reader a lack of awareness of the obviously distorted nature of their thinking (Shneidman and Farberow, 1957). Suicide notes are often full of irrelevant details as though the writer was incapable of distinguishing important from trite information (Tripodes, 1976). Unconscious dynamics and religious moral values are sometimes alluded to, suggesting deeper motivations for their action (Leenaars and Balance, 1984b).

Demographic details

Many studies have examined demographic variations in suicide notes (e.g. Darbonne, 1969). Since suicide is a heterogeneous behaviour, it is logical to assume that the reasons and circumstances surrounding an elderly suicide would differ from those of an adolescent suicide and these would be manifest in the note. A lifespan approach is important in suicidology, especially because suicide afflicts all age groups.

Age and sex

Suicide notes are more often left by younger individuals and notes written by men more often mention depression and poor health as reasons for suicide (Lester and Heim, 1992). Men are more likely to mention physical pain, interpersonal friction and psychological pain. The fact that there are few sex differences has led some to conclude that the psychological determinants of suicide in men and women are not substantially different (Leenaars, 1988b). However, a large study of suicide notes in the former West Berlin has reported substantial gender differences: women were more likely to leave notes. Furthermore, elderly people were more likely to leave notes than young people (contrary to Capstick's (1960) finding), and widowed were more likely than single or divorced people. Those individuals who had experienced the death of a partner or who appeared to embrace philosophical motives for committing suicide also left notes more often. Very few mentally ill people left notes which may reduce the ability to generalize findings from suicide note analysis, or it may simply be that the mentally ill are less lucid or communicative than others.

Darbonne (1969) was interested in identifying differences in the age of the writers and the content of suicide notes. He categorized the notes according to five sub-sections: (1) addressee of the suicide note, (2) reasons for suicide, (3) affect indicated in note, (4) specific content other than affect and (5) general focus of the note. The reasons for suicide and the general focus of the suicide note were significantly related to age. Young adults (aged 20–39) more often gave reasons such as feelings of rejection and problems with, or competition for, heterosexual objects of love. They were unlikely to mention physical illness or pain, possibly because they are statistically less likely to have suffered physical illness than older people. Middle-aged people (aged 40–49) more often expressed feelings of being overwhelmed by the demands of life and were tired or bored and wanted a way out. This group often looked to an afterlife for comfort. The 50–59-year-olds who left notes were least likely to give a reason but rather used the note to convey instructions and other factual information. Finally, the oldest group (60+ years) often tried to answer the 'why' question and were more likely to cite pain, illness, physical disability, loneliness and isolation as reasons for suicide. Since this group had lived longest they also tended to be more tired of life than any other age groups.

Interpreting the significance of age-related differences in suicide notes has been hampered by inconsistencies in the classification of people into young, middle-aged and old. To overcome this problem, Leenaars (1989) proposed a universal classification system based on Erikson's (1968) model of developmental stages: young adulthood (18–25), middle adulthood (25–55) and late adulthood (55 and above). While there is much to be said for adopting a common age classification system there is little evidence that researchers are moving in this direction.

As the age of the suicidal person increases, both the desire to die and the desire to kill decrease (Shneidman and Farberow, 1957). Lester and Hummel (1980) found that older people who commit suicide tend to be more direct and explicit about wanting to take their own lives.

Several authors have noted that younger people are less likely to show feelings or emotion in comparison to older suicides (Lester and Reeve, 1982; Tuckman, Kleiner and Lavell, 1959). There are also substantial sex by age interactions across the adult life span, including differences in perturbation, relationships, self-cognition and long-term instability (Leenaars, 1987). In particular, young and middle-aged adults exhibit greater confusion about their self-cognition than elderly people and are more preoccupied with relationships. Young women are often more preoccupied with their inability to develop or maintain 'constructive tendencies' than same-age men.

Relatively little attention has been paid to the suicide notes of adolescents. One small-scale study analysed the suicide notes left by 17 adolescents (aged 10–19) in Montreal, Canada (Posener et al., 1989). Notes were scored on 11 suicide variables, established through an analysis of the published literature, including psychotic disorganization, aggression and ambivalence. The results partially replicated previous findings with adults: ambivalent attachment, loss of a love object, internalization, and self-directed aggression were all evident in the notes.

Simulated suicide note analysis

Shneidman and Farberow (1957) also pioneered comparisons between genuine and simulated suicide notes. A simulated suicide note (SSN) is a communication written by someone who is not suicidal but who has been instructed to write a note as if they were. These notes are matched according to demographic variables and compared with genuine suicide notes. Any differences that emerge are attributed to differences in suicidality and characteristics that discriminate between these two groups are warranted in any explanation of suicide.

This methodology has been criticized on several grounds. In Shneidman and Farberow's (1957) original study the simulated note writers (SNWs) were pre-tested or screened using a personality test and assessment of psychological history. Those who were prone to depression were excluded from the study, prompting some critics to conclude that the exclusion criterion fundamentally flawed the findings (e.g. Black, 1993). For example, any differences reported by Shneidman and Farberow could have been due to differences in psychological stability between the two samples. Hence, in his own study Black did not use a pre-selection procedure and all SNWs were asked to 'write a suicide note you would write as if you were going to take your own life' (Black, 1993). There were no significant differences between the genuine note writers and the non-note-writing suicide completers in terms of sex, age, marital status, occupational level, employment status, place of death, or method of suicide. Black also replicated Shneidman and Farberow's (1957) finding that genuine notes are significantly longer than simulations. Black argued that the pre-selection procedure used in the 1957 study produced a group of SNWs who were extremely good role players. Genuine note writers (GNWs) gave more instructions, more factual information, cited more original ideas and more frequently dated the note.

Diamond and colleagues (1995) argued that Black made no mention of how he thought his correction (i.e. no pre-selection) would affect his results nor how he defined and operationalized the constructs of psychological stability. Diamond concluded that 'because Black offered no theory and is testing no hypotheses, the results are not interpretable'. This is perhaps a little harsh and demonstrates the lack of agreement about the usefulness of simulation studies. It is probably safer to say that it is difficult to interpret the differences in genuine and simulated suicide notes and the value of the technique has yet to be firmly established.

Thematic Guide to Suicide Prediction

The Thematic Guide to Suicide Prediction (TGSP) was developed by Antoon Leenaars in order to explain suicide psychologically within a personality framework. Leenaars argued that much of suicide note analysis was atheoretical and he sought to address this problem within an empirical framework. He generated a list of a hundred protocol sentences derived from the theories of ten suicidologists: Alfred Adler, Ludwig Binswanger, Sigmund Freud, Carl G. Jung, Karl A. Menninger, George Kelly, Henry A. Murray, Edwin S. Shneidman, Harry Stack Sullivan and George Zilboorg. Essentially, he brought together the formulations and postulations of these leaders in the field of suicidology and applied them to suicide notes. Twenty-three of the protocol sentences were found to be present in two-thirds of the genuine suicide notes that he sampled. He concluded that these were, by implication, the common psychological characteristics of suicide. Furthermore, he found that 18 protocol sentences were found significantly more often in genuine as opposed to simulated notes. These sentences were then grouped statistically into eight discrete clusters. This gave rise to the Thematic Guide to Suicide Prediction (TGSP) and a subsequent modification (Leenaars, 1996) intended to improve its usefulness in the prediction and prevention of suicide.

The TGSP (Table 6.1) is divided into two sections: intrapsychic and interpersonal clusters. Leenaars takes the view that suicidal behaviour is a product of intrapsychic factors and the way individuals interact with their environment.

82

Table 6.1 The eight clusters of the Thematic Guide to Suicide Prediction

Intrapsychic	Interpersonal
Unbearable psychological pain	Interpersonal relations
Cognitive constriction	Rejection – aggression
Indirect expressions	Identification – egression
Inability to adjust	
Ego	

Source TGSP, Leenaars (1996)

The intrapsychic components (clusters) of the TGSP

Unbearable psychological pain

This refers to an unendurable psychological pain (Shneidman, 1985): 'it is the pain of feeling pain' (Leenaars, 1996). Suicidal people feel hopeless, helpless and boxed in. Unbearable psychological pain (UPP) was present in more than 90 per cent of one sample of suicide notes (O'Connor et al., 1999a). The suicidal person often feels they have lost interest in life and sees suicide as the only solution. They may feel unwilling or unable to meet life's challenges and desire an urgent, permanent solution – death. A typical expression of unbearable psychological pain is illustrated by a 30-year-old married man whose wife asked for a trial separation prior to his suicide:

I have lost any happiness in life
lost any love in life and
can no longer take the pain of
losing you and the kids...
I'm sorry I hurt you but it wasn't true
what I said

Cognitive constriction

Often referred to as 'tunnel vision', and described in earlier chapters, this is a salient attribute of the suicidal mind. The individual seems to be incapable of perceiving his or her situation in a logical, rational manner. To others the suicidal person seems unaware that their thought processes are constricted and clouded by overwhelming emotion. For example, a 45-year-old man, completely intoxicated and overwhelmed with hate communicates thus to the recipient of the note:

> *Well you all win.*
> *It no longer matters what I wasn't or how I*
> *want to sort my life out.*
> *Hole in ground will do....don't wear black.*

O'Connor et al. (1999a) found evidence of cognitive constriction in nearly 90 per cent of their sample of suicide notes.

Indirect expressions

This cluster is characterized by ambivalence. The person experiences powerful contradictory emotions and is 'torn' between deciding which to follow. For example, one woman wrote:

> *[name of intended recipient] right now I feel extreme*
> *hate for you but in 1 minute I was telling you that I love you,*
> *I'm sorry, why me?*

Contradictory emotions are often most evident in a conflict between love and hate of others as well as a sense of indecision over whether to choose life or death.

Inability to adjust

It seems that it is not simply the situation *per se* which renders people at risk but rather the perception that they are incapable of adjusting to the demands that are placed on them. A mental disorder may promote maladjustment and hence amplify feelings of being unable to adapt. Inability to adjust may be communicated in many ways. One example is that of a divorced man aged 50, who argued that there was no justification for continuing with life:

> *How can I begin.*
> *I can only say the time has come*
> *to say goodbye. My life is not worth*
> *living, as I have nothing to live for.*
> *All I seem to do is worry and feel depressed.*
> *I have no motivation to carry on...*

Ego

Psychodynamic in origin, this cluster is concerned with the weakness we sometimes feel when we cannot develop constructive tendencies. The suicidal person is thought to have difficulties in developing love or attachment relationships with someone close to him or her. In addition, the act of suicide may be construed as self-punishment for some traumatic past event. O'Connor et al. (1999a) found that communications related to the ego cluster were evident in 36 per cent of suicide notes in their sample.

The interpersonal components of the TGSP

Interpersonal relations

The suicidal individual has difficulty establishing or maintaining relationships with others. This is similar to the intrapsychic component – ego – but is extended to include situations where a positive development or a solution seems unobtainable. In this case, the suicide is related to frustrated needs concerning an attachment relationship. Problems associated with interpersonal relations have been detected in up to 75 per cent of suicide notes (O'Connor et al., 1999a).

Rejection–aggression

The rejection-aggression hypothesis – suicide is an aggressive outcome caused by intolerable levels of frustration – has a long history within the psychoanalytic tradition. Many key thinkers on suicide have put forward similar hypotheses to this at one time or another: loss or abandonment is thought to promote feelings of rejection which in turn culminate in aggression that is directed inward.

Identification–egression

Freud (1920/1974) hypothesized that identifying with a lost or rejecting person is central to understanding the suicidal mind. When key emotional needs are not satisfied the person experiences discomfort, wants to flee (egress) from their intolerable situation and comes to view suicide as the solution. One young man communicated this feeling of self-hate when in reality he appears to have been angry with other people:

My life has been ruined by so many people...
Oh how I hate myself, I have really wrecked your life...

Usefulness of TGSP

Relatively few independent studies of suicide notes have used the TGSP framework. An exception is O'Connor et al. (1999a) who examined 45 suicide notes drawn from a catchment sample of 142 suicides taken from three regions in Northern Ireland. These notes were rated

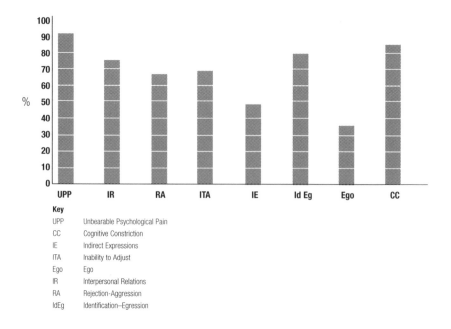

Figure 6.1 Distribution of TGSP cluster themes in suicide notes (n=45)

for the presence of the protocol sentences in the Thematic Guide to Suicide Prediction (TGSP). An innovative feature of this study is the manner in which the analysis of the notes was undertaken within a wider psychosocial context provided by the coroners' inquest papers. The notes were read by three psychologists who had access to information contained in the coroners' inquest papers and used that information to code each note. O'Connor et al. found substantial evidence for the presence of protocol clusters in the suicide notes (see Figure 6.1).

O'Connor et al. found that note writers did not differ from those who did not leave a note in terms of age, marital status or social class. The majority of those who killed themselves were young or middle-aged, and this pattern was repeated in the group who left notes. Almost 90 per cent were either single or married at the time of death and most were manually skilled. They used Erikson's age categories as recommended by Leenaars and found no significant differences of protocol clusters across age – the psychological profile for each of the eight clusters was similar for young, middle and late adulthood. This is surprising because motivations for suicide are known to differ across the lifespan. Leenaars (1989) reported that younger adults differ

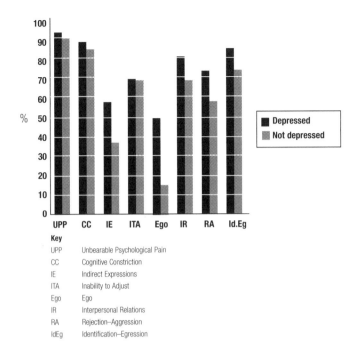

Key

UPP	Unbearable Psychological Pain
CC	Cognitive Constriction
IE	Indirect Expressions
ITA	Inability to Adjust
Ego	Ego
IR	Interpersonal Relations
RA	Rejection–Aggression
IdEg	Identification–Egression

Reproduced with permission from *Crisis* © 1999 Hogrefe & Huber Publishers (O'Connor et. al., 1999a)

Figure 6.2 Distribution of clusters across depressed and not depressed note writers

psychologically from older adults: they more often recounted details of disturbed, unbearable interpersonal situations than the older suicides. O'Connor et al. found some evidence for this in their sample but the difference was not statistically significant. Leenaars also found identification–egression to be more prevalent in young adults than in older adults. O'Connor et al. found more young adults referred to identification–egression issues than middle-aged adults but no more so than older adults. Leenaars observed ego protocol sentences more often in the suicide notes of young adults. O'Connor et al. also found young adults more frequently recorded problems with constructive tendencies although the trend in their data was not statistically significant.

Depressed and non-depressed note writers

Depressed people kill themselves for different reasons than non-depressed people. Thus, O'Connor et al. predicted that the manifest content of suicide notes authored by depressed and non-depressed people should be different (see Figure 6.2). In their sample 36 per cent of the note writers were defined as depressed. Depressed note writers (50 per cent) were significantly more likely to communicate problems within the ego cluster than the non-depressed comparisons (16 per cent). One depressed 59-year-old man communicated his failure and inability to develop and maintain constructive attachments with his partner thus:

> *To my dear XXXX*
> *Please forgive me taking this way out.*
> *I am sorry* [for] *the hard life you have had.*
> *If I had the chance again, I would be much better to you.*
> *You deserve the best, sorry I could not do that for you*
> *...I really loved you in my own way...*

O'Connor et al. found that unbearable psychological pain did not distinguish between depressed and non-depressed notes. However, depressed note writers were significantly more preoccupied with their inability to develop constructive tendencies. Thirty per cent of depressed note writers communicated this as a contributory factor to the suicide compared with only 5 per cent of those who were not depressed.

Other individual protocol sentences within the clusters seemed to be important in distinguishing between these groups. Two of the cog-

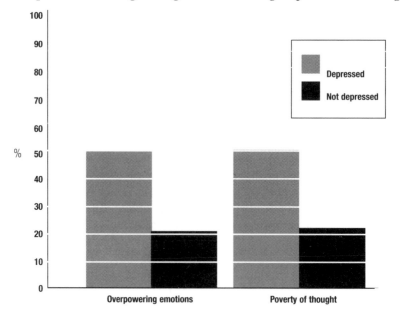

Reproduced with permission from *Crisis* © *1999 Hogrefe & Huber Publishers*

Figure 6.3 Cognitive constriction protocol sentences which discriminated depressed from not depressed suicide notes (O'Connor et al., 1999a)

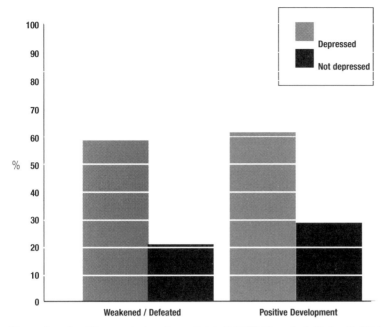

Figure 6.4 Interpersonal protocol sentences which discriminated depressed from not depressed suicide notes

nitive constriction protocols were significantly overrepresented among the depressed note writers (see Figure 6.3). Depressed suicides were more likely to communicate feelings of overpowering emotion, constricted logic and perception. For example, a single 29-year-old male was so preoccupied with illness and suffering that he entrusted himself to God:

> *Free me from this illness and pain if you will,*
> [and] *if it be for my good.*
> *You love me too much to let me suffer*
> *unless it be for my good.*
> *Therefore, O Lord, I trust myself to you;*
> *do with me as you please...*

O'Connor et al. also reported underlying reasons for suicide in about one-third of the depressed notes, whereas none of the notes written by those considered not to be depressed conveyed any sense of an unconscious dynamic to their actions. Depressed suicide note writers were also more likely to communicate problems associated with interpersonal relations. About half of the depressed suicide note writers reported being weakened or defeated by unresolved interpersonal problems compared with only 21 per cent of those who were not depressed. An extreme example is the case of a 45-year-old married man who was in an abusive relationship which he could not control:

> *I said that I lived from day to day but I cannot live with myself*
> [for what] *I did yesterday*
> *I have lived with an obsession this last few weeks which has divided us – please, please forgive me my darling for that....*
> *I have lost all that love and life could never be the same again.*

They also found depressed people to be less likely to perceive any positive outcomes to their troubled relationships. In short, if the relationship appears to be irreconcilable the individual sees no other option but to end their life (Figure 6.4).

Note-writing and previous suicidal attempts

People who kill themselves and who are known to have a history of suicidal behaviour have different psychosocial profiles from those without a history of previous attempts. Surprisingly, there have been few attempts to explore this relationship in note-writing. O'Connor et al. found almost one-third of their sample of suicide note writers had attempted suicide at least once before. However, those with a history of self-harm were no more likely to write a suicide note than those who completed at the first attempt. They found the ego cluster to be the only one which was significantly more often communicated in the notes of those with a history of self-harm than those without a self-harm history. The other seven clusters were well represented but were not differentially associated with previous attempts. Four individual protocols distinguished repeaters from first-time completers (see Table 6.2).

Table 6.2 Individual protocol sentences that distinguish suicide note writers with and without previous attempt history

Protocol sentence	History of previous attempt (per cent)	No previous attempt (per cent)
Aggression has been turned inward	64.3	25.8
Exhibits a serious disorder in adjustment	85.7	51.6
Appears to be aggressive towards someone else	35.7	9.7
Unwilling to accept the pain of loss	14.3	48.4

Source: O'Connor et al., 1999a

The previous attempt group was more likely than first-time completers to communicate the suicide act as aggression turned inward. This may be illustrated in the case of a young man who blamed himself:

Oh how I hate myself, I have really wrecked your life, and don't say that's no[t] true. I've stopped you from doing X-amount of things, I hate myself so much.

In another letter he expressed his absolute distress at losing his partner:

XXXXX I'm hopeless without you, please don't leave me

O'Connor et al. also observed serious disorder of adjustment in 85 per cent of their sample of self-harmers compared with only half of those without a history of self-harm. They found some evidence of aggression directed against other people in the notes of those with a history of self-harm. For example, a young man warned in his note:

... the day when you told me you would phone me I kind of knew you wouldnt...
I told you I could not live without you I meant it.

They found this type of aggression was rarely communicated by those who had no history of self-harm. They also found that first-time completers were more likely than those with a history of self-harm to be unwilling to accept the pain of losing an ideal or loved one.

Why do people who are not depressed commit suicide?

Depressed suicide is certainly distinct from non-depressed suicide but there have been few attempts to examine the psychological profiles of these two sub-groups. This may in part be due to the deterring influence of a widely held presumption that depression must be present in every case of suicide and that it is simply undetected in a proportion. However, O'Connor et al. found that some psychological correlates, as measured by the TGSP, of depressed suicide differ from non-depressed suicide. The suicide notes of those who are depressed suggest the writer has greater difficulty developing and maintaining constructive tendencies. This may be explained by the fact that depressed individuals find it difficult to use the interpersonal skills

d to foster strong attachment relationships. They find it diffi-
like themselves and even more difficult to love others.

ιcide note analysis also suggests that those with discrete symp-
ι of depression can become intoxicated with overpowering emo-
ιs and this may be mediated by depressed affect. Individuals may
ιte on those aspects of their lives that are causing distress and this
ιιxation may precipitate further depression and overwhelming emotional distress. This emotional intoxication may also be related to cognitive constriction and poverty of thought. O'Connor et al. found
unresolved interpersonal problems were less frequent among the non-
depressed suicides and they were also less likely to manifest high
levels of cognitive constriction.

The TGSP has been useful in detecting some aspects of the psychological profile of those who leave suicide letters. In particular it has
clarified the role of some aspects of cognitive functioning possibly
amenable to change that potentially could prevent some suicides. The
TGSP has also shown that first-time suicides differ psychologically
from those with a history of previous attempts. Earlier studies
(Kreitman and Foster, 1991) suggested that those who repeatedly
attempt suicide are more aggressive than those who only attempt
once. O'Connor et al.'s analysis of suicide notes supports that conjec-
ture: those with a history of attempted suicide communicated in ways
that conveyed more aggression to others as well as to themselves.
Therapies aimed at coping with aggression may be an important intervention strategy. It may be that some form of expressive therapy might
benefit those parasuicidal people who present at general hospitals and
require follow-up treatment.

Conclusion

Suicide is a very difficult behaviour to predict and therefore to prevent. Moreover, a well-concealed plan for suicide will almost always
succeed. Tools like the TGSP may have considerable constructive
validity and should be more widely used in the identification of at-risk
individuals. Furthermore, the underlying psychological processes (e.g.
cognitive constriction) must be treated specifically and not viewed
only as products of other gross disorders. Suicide notes can only tell us
a limited amount and they must be used in conjunction with other
methodologies both to off set inherent methodological limitations and
to provide a more comprehensive picture. For example, the integration
of suicide analysis, interviews with families and interviews with
attempters would be more effective in psychological profiling. Suicide
notes have been shown to be helpful in the profiling of suicide and the
knowledge obtained requires more extensive dissemination among

healthcare practitioners. In the next chapter, we consider another form of communication – deliberate self-harm.

Chapter review

- Suicide notes, when examined in the context of the deceased's life history, are invaluable tools for understanding suicide.
- Suicide notes contain a variety of information relating to the death including: situational factors, relationship factors, emotional factors and psychological factors.
- Age differences are found among note writers. This is not surprising as young people kill themselves for different reasons than older people.
- The Thematic Guide to Suicide Prediction (TGSP) is a useful tool for identifying the intrapsychic and interpersonal components of suicidal communication.
- Depressed suicides, as communicated in suicide notes, tend to have greater difficulty developing and maintaining relationships than non-depressed suicides.
- Those who have a history of previous attempt communicate more feelings of aggression than those who kill themselves at their first attempt.
- If suicide notes were studied more widely then we might get closer to understanding why different people commit suicide, and hence prevent needless deaths.

7
Suicide Communication II: Parasuicide

Parasuicide is a serious public health problem and one of the most frequent causes for admission to Accident and Emergency departments. As many as 120,000 patients are admitted annually to general hospitals in England and Wales with self-inflicted injuries (Hawton and Fagg, 1992). Women are admitted more often than men and the incidence of self-injurious behaviour is relatively rare in those under the age of 16. However, there has been a large increase in the incidence of parasuicide among 15–19-year-olds. Why this should be is not clear and the increase among this age group would not have been predicted by any of the major theories of suicide. The impact of self-harming on medical workloads has been illustrated in an economic analysis of the cost of treating 44 repeat parasuicide patients admitted to the Royal Infirmary of Edinburgh: 'the estimated costs solely associated with hospital accommodation and psychiatric assessment of the present sample during follow-up were £34,036.30 (1986–1987 prices)' (Rodger and Scott, 1995).

Differences between first-timers and repeaters

In Chapter 3 we examined some of the clinical factors discriminating between those who attempt suicide for the first time and repeaters. Comparative studies of differences between people who attempt suicide once and those who make repeated attempts indicate that the latter are more likely to:

- be unemployed;
- be in financial difficulty;
- have a criminal record;
- have a history of contact with psychiatric services;
- be divorced, separated or living alone;
- be in violent relationships;

- lack social support networks
- exhibit relatively diminished levels of general psychosocial functioning.

A prospective study conducted in Nottingham followed deliberate self-poisoners for a year after the first episode. Those who repeated were more likely to be aged between 25 and 54, to have ingested more than one drug, to report a previous episode of self-poisoning and to have been in psychiatric care (Owens et al., 1994).

Gupta et al. (1995) compared the clinical and social profiles of 42 first-timers with 39 repeaters. Those who made repeated suicide attempts had experienced more marital breakdown, were more likely to be involved in a violent relationship and had had more contact with psychiatric services. They also found that those who made repeated attempts at suicide were more likely to say that they did *not* wish to die and this may partly account for the popular view that those who make a failed attempt at suicide are not serious about taking their own lives but are making a desperate request for assistance. This view is in fact a myth. Those who make repeated attempts at suicide are not 'merely' seeking help by drawing attention to their difficulties. They are very likely to kill themselves at a later date (Suokas and Lonnqvist, 1991). Understanding the psychological differences between repeaters and first-timers has important implications for primary healthcare and prevention.

Between 40 and 50 per cent of all parasuicide admissions are repeat episodes (Platt et al., 1988). Some estimate that between one-half and two-thirds of all those who attempt suicide repeat the attempt (Bille-Brahe and Jessen, 1994b). That these individuals have already presented to the healthcare team at the first episode suggests that the service provided may not be particularly effective at ameliorating the factors that drove them to attempt suicide. In order to understand why this might be it is important to examine what it is people say about their actions and how they communicate their explanations to others. However, there have been surprisingly few studies of communication between those classified as 'parasuicides' and healthcare teams. There is a variety of reasons for this. First, the label 'parasuicide' is not diagnostically precise and refers to a very broad range of self-harming behaviours. A majority of hospital-admitted non-fatal acts of self-injury are not strictly defined as attempts at suicide. To some extent this has deterred researchers from investigating such a heterogeneous group of people (see Chapter 2 for a review). Second, those who might be described as 'parasuicidal' can be particularly elusive and frequently evade the attention of healthcare staff. They may do this for a variety of reasons: they may feel embarrassed or 'stupid' about what they have done; they may wish to avoid detection because they consider their actions to have been impulsive and out of character; or they may regard what they did as an inappropriate solution to a problem that is now behind them.

What self-harmers say

In order to obtain a more complete picture of what self-harmers say about themselves, O'Connor et al. (2000) conducted detailed interviews with 50 people admitted to the observational ward of a general hospital in Belfast. Almost all were in their thirties and the majority (60 per cent) were women; 42 per cent were married and 32 per cent were single. Analgesics, anxiolytics and antidepressants were implicated in over 70 per cent of the attempts although analgesics – usually paracetamol – were most often taken in combination with other drugs and alcohol.

Attributions to psychological well-being

O'Connor et al. (2000) argue that suicide and parasuicide reside on a continuum and that the outcome of a suicide attempt – life or death – cannot be used to retrospectively differentiate the psychological profiles of those who attempt, from those who complete suicide. Thus, the content of their interview schedule related to five major domains of completed suicide:

- psychological well-being;
- physical health;
- changes in behaviour;
- major stressors;
- social support and control in life.

Their interviews with those who had attempted suicide focused on feelings of depression, optimism, lethargy, anxiety and thoughts about suicide. They found no significant gender differences in self-perceptions of psychological well-being. One-third associated their suicidal actions with their emergence from a bout of utterly debilitating depression. This supports the speculations made in some retrospective studies of suicide that those suffering from depression may be at increased risk towards the end of an episode because they possess sufficient energy to make an attempt on their own life. When people are profoundly depressed and overwhelmed by a sense of hopelessness they may formulate a solution based on suicide. The availability of a potential solution may ameliorate their despair, leading to a reduced sense of lethargy that may, paradoxically, motivate the person to see through their suicidal solution.

O'Connor et al. also found that the causes of depression were frequently attributed to interpersonal problems. More importantly these attributions were often made in a manner that conveyed a sense of confusion and ambivalence reminiscent of messages left in suicide notes. For example, a 21 year-old woman who had been cohabiting with her ex-boyfriend attributed her suicide attempt to his actions:

> *I broke-up with my boyfriend of about one and a half years. We were living together, everything was great, then he went funny. Anyway, he did the dirt on me. But I broke it off, he was older than me......I obviously could not see any future with him, not after what he done, I just don't see any future at all, I just feel depressed more and more.*

While the young woman saw a direct link between the break-up and her depression, she also offered a great deal of additional information – in no particular order or significance – that implicates factors to do with the duration of the relationship, their cohabiting, the way she was cheated, her termination of the relationship, their age difference and the prospect of a bleak future.

Another example is that of a 44-year-old woman who had taken a huge overdose of diazepam and prozac following a recent separation from her husband:

> *Yeah, I have been on antidepressants for about 6 years, they are rubbish. My husband is having an affair, I've known about it for about 6 months. But these last few weeks it has really been getting me down, getting from bad to worse. I wish I could simply switch off, pretend that I did not care, then I wouldn't feel so fed-up or depressed ...*

The relationship failure and subsequent depression are reported as important determinants of her suicidal action. References are made to a complex web of interwoven factors, specifically the failure of three ways of coping: medication, dissociation and denial. Here is a person who has indicated that she made at least three genuine attempts to resolve her problems. In this context her suicide attempt could be regarded as highly adaptive in the sense that it is a drastic resolution attempted only after others had failed.

The reasons cited as the cause of depression that lead to a suicide attempt can be varied. They can include a general inability to cope, problems with sexuality, concerns with weight, problems at work and being in trouble with the law. O'Connor et al. found that almost all of the 50 people they interviewed were not hopeful for the future. This sense of futility is perhaps best illustrated by the words of a 24-year-old married woman:

> *What is the point in going on, everything I do is wrong, I don't look forward to tomorrow or the next day. My husband is fed-up listening to me, he thinks there is nothing wrong with me, I have gone past bothering or caring...*

The most significant part of this comment is in the phrase *'he thinks there is nothing wrong with me'*. Suicidal thinking is particularly cruel because it is invisible – those who feel suicidal do not bear any obvious marks nor do they usually manifest such obvious changes that allow others to immediately recognize what it is they are feeling. The suicidal person will often wish they could point to their demonstrable difference from others – a difference that might reveal their sense that 'everything is wrong with me'.

O'Connor et al. found that this sense that others do not notice – and therefore do not care – permeated many of their interviews. For example, they found that only one-third of their sample would consider going to their GP if they were feeling anxious or depressed. GPs are always professionally and personally disturbed by the loss of a patient through suicide. However just as the physician cannot easily detect whether someone may be contemplating suicide, neither can the suicidal person recognize that their sense of isolation and despair may be invisible to those who care. This sense of isolation experienced by those who attempt suicide is illustrated in several interviews recorded by O'Connor et al.

> *I went to the doctor, he just looks at you, he's good like but he didn't do anything to help . It's not like he did not do anything but like he cannot do anything.*

> *I didn't think you could go [to GP] about things like that [depression], I thought it was just for medical reasons.*

> *I don't like talking to them. No I can't be bothered with them. They think they are so much better than you. They couldn't care less.*

Attributions to physical health

> *My back pain interferes with everything that I do, my everyday duties. It makes me feel terrible, I have to get up if I am sitting, I have to sit down if I am standing. It is really irritating, I feel like crying half the time, it gets me really down.*

Physical illness is an important contributory factor in many completed suicides but is not as conspicuous among those who have attempted to take their own lives. Among parasuicides physical well-being is implicated in equal measure by men and women, although some studies report that men are more likely to reveal concerns about physical health and more often perceive their physical health as interfering with their everyday life (O'Connor et al., 2000). O'Connor et al also found that while 67 per cent of their sample were on medication for physical ailments only 42 per cent thought that it was having any beneficial effects. Among those who were depressed, almost one-third thought that their physical condition played any role in their depression. Pain associated with a physical ailment was most frequently given as the reason why physical health interfered with everyday life.

Changes in behaviour

A history of self-harm is a common characteristic of both men and women who attempt suicide. O'Connor et al. (2000) found that the average interval between the last parasuicidal episode and the most recent was 23 months. They also found that men and women were equally likely to refer to changes in behaviour prior to their suicide attempt. The majority had changed their sleeping (86 per cent) and eating (72 per cent) habits in the weeks prior to the attempt and more than half (56 per cent) had changed their drinking habits. One-third suffered from nightmares and 18 per cent reported that they were dependent on alcohol to get them through the day. A large percentage of men (65 per cent) and women (70 per cent) reported going out less often. Thus, in the days leading up to their attempt the parasuicidal person experiences a number of subtle changes in basic physiological activity. Their increased social isolation reduces the likelihood that others will notice these changes. It seems likely that changes in sleeping, eating and drinking are unnoticed by others in the days leading up to the suicide attempt and that it is only with the benefit of hindsight that the cumulative effect of the changes can be seen.

O'Connor et al. also found that half of those interviewed felt that their outlook on life had changed between the night before (pre-parasuicide) and the morning after the attempt. These changes were usually to do with a sense of relief at still being alive:

> *I don't want to die and leave my children without a mummy, I am so glad nothing happened to me.* (a young mother)

Nevertheless, the other half said their feelings were unchanged from the night before, some still wishing they were dead. This in itself is an important indication of the personal meaning attached to the attempt and reflects the low value placed on personal existence:

> *No, nothing has changed, I don't care, I feel the same way as I did last night. Sure, nothing has changed, has it? I feel as depressed and useless as I did yesterday.* (middle-aged man)

The language used by those who have attempted suicide may contain messages that are easily overlooked. Many report feeling 'stupid' or 'guilty' about what they did:

> *I feel stupid for what I did. It has only made things worse for me, I feel worse. How could I have done this to my family, how stupid was I? I feel so guilty, I have hurt all my friends as well. How can I face them, what will they think of me?*

It is all too easy to offer words of agreement – 'yes, it was a stupid thing to do, what must you have been thinking to have done this?' – intended to support the person through their recovery. But these may do more harm than good because the key message is that the person's sense of self-worth is further diminished and agreement can be readily interpreted as tacit reinforcement for the person's self-view as bad and mad.

Vacillations in mood and conflicting emotions are a feature of many suicide notes. They are also evident in emotional responses after a suicide attempt: many report feeling both angry and relieved, suggesting the oscillations in mood that preceded their attempt had not diminished and that ambivalence remains a salient feature of their feelings about themselves. The confusions and contradictions in suicidal thinking are vividly illustrated by the fact that the vast majority of those who attempt suicide report that they knew precisely what they were doing. However, not all those who realize they are risking their lives say they want to die. O'Connor et al. found that 70 per cent of their sample said they had wanted to die at the time of the attempt but this reduced to 46 per cent when asked if they still wanted to die (post-parasuicide). The fact that nearly one half still wanted to die the day following the suicide attempt conveys an important message: one would be wrong to think that a failed suicide attempt marks a significant threshold that 'changes everything' for the person. About half of the people interviewed felt that nothing had changed at all and that in itself is an important indicator of the significance they attach to the event and to themselves.

Suicidal behaviour has always been defined as an aggressive act, although it is not always 'self-murder' in the traditional sense. The majority of those who have attempted suicide describe their actions as aggressive, but many interpret the episode as directed primarily against someone else, usually a partner, rather than themselves. In some circumstances the motive may be revenge although parasuicidal acts are more often motivated by a need to highlight intolerable experiences and to gain temporary relief. For example, O'Connor et al. reported that 20 per cent implicated interpersonal problems in the suicide attempt and in many cases these were part of the 'intolerable situation'. Interpersonal circumstances were often interpreted as meaningless or troublesome. For example, a 33-year-old man wanted to end his life because he could no longer endure the psychological pain:

> *I just had enough, I just wanted to end it all, I just couldn't take it any more. I have been feeling down since the stabbing incident, it still torments me, I have no interest in life and I don't want to leave the house...*

Perceptions of major stressors

It is hardly surprising that the vast majority of those who talk about their suicide attempt consider their lives to be enormously stressful. The stressors reported can be enormously varied. They range from relationship problems to divorce and from being in trouble with the law to being a perpetrator or a victim of sexual abuse. Interpersonal problems are the most frequently cited stressors, followed by work-related stress and financial problems (O'Connor et al., 2000). These stressors typically interacted: work-related stress led to unemployment which brought additional financial problems and these in turn soured relationships with spouses, partners and family members. Those who drink to relax or to gain a (false) sense of control over their problems tend to drink more when under pressure; and in using alcohol as a coping strategy they add to their financial difficulties. Alcohol abuse further diminishes the quality of their relationships with family and friends.

O'Connor et al. found that a little over half of their sample said that, in general, they could see solutions to their problems, although one-third felt they were unable to see solutions to their problems at the time of the attempt. Many found it difficult to relax. Watching television was the most frequently used method of relaxation, although in many cases this proved to be little more than a temporary diversion. Almost everyone who attempts suicide describes themselves as unable to relax; and while most also believe that they worry unnecessarily, they feel unable to control bouts of catastrophic worrying.

O'Connor et al. found only a small percentage of their sample expressed their suicidal intentions before their attempt or made preparations so as not to be found. Such preparations usually involved locking the room or house where the attempt was to take place or over-dosing when no-one was expected to arrive on the scene. The method of parasuicide chosen was most often a matter of pragmatics. Many overdose on drugs that are readily to hand and are not particularly selective about what they ingest.

Perceptions of social support/control in life

Parasuicidal episodes are especially difficult to endure because suicidal actions and thoughts are profoundly debilitating – most people who attempt suicide feel little sense of control over their own lives – but largely invisible and intangible. For example, while a parasuicide episode is associated with increased social isolation, the majority of those who attempt suicide regard themselves are affable and outgoing – they are not conspicuously introverted or withdrawn. The vast majority also report having close friends in whom they can confide yet described themselves as feeling very lonely, often when there were others around them. Thus, the majority feel themselves to be psychologically, as distinct from socially, isolated (O'Connor et al., 2000).

Friends can provide an invaluable source of social and personal support but even these may be unable to help someone work through a parasuicidal episode. The family physician can be an important source of professional assistance but may often be perceived as less competent to assist with affective problems than with physical ailments. More importantly, O'Connor et al. found that although a majority of their sample said they would do something to solve a physical ailment (e.g. take medication or go to the doctor), less than half said that they would do *anything* to resolve an affective problem. Many took the view that the problem would simply go away.

First-time and repeat parasuicides

It is likely that those who attempt suicide for the first time are different from those who make repeated attempts. Demographic variables such as age and gender do not discriminate between these two groups. O'Connor et al. (2000) examined in detail replies elicited against Likert-type scales and included them in a discriminant function analysis to determine which variables discriminated the first-timers from the repeaters. The questions were organized into sub-scales according to the five risk factor domains considered in the interviews they conducted: psychological well-being, physical health, changes in behaviour, perceptions of major stressors and perceptions of social support and control in life. Interestingly, there were very few significant differences between those with and without a history of self-harm across any of the interview items. However, the repeat parasuicide group tended to be less relieved, more angry, realize the risk they had taken and were more likely to view the attempt as aggressive.

Communicating a desire to die

O'Connor et al. (2000) also compared those who, when interviewed, were still expressing a desire to die – these they termed 'verbalizers' – with those who said they did not want to die ('non-verbalizers') and those who were uncertain about whether they wanted to live or die ('ambivalents'). They found that the verbalizers were significantly less likely to be relieved at being alive than the other two groups. All of the ambivalents were relieved to be alive and 82 per cent of those who did not want to die were relieved compared with 38 per cent of the verbalizers. All of the verbalizers and ambivalents said that they understood the risks associated with their actions compared with nearly two-thirds of the non-verbalizers. Those who wanted to die were least likely to feel that confiding in others did any good. All of the verbalizers reported that the opinion that they held of themselves had changed prior to the attempt but the non-verbalizers were least likely to have changed their self-opinion in the time before the parasuicidal episode.

Surprisingly, the ambivalent group were *more* relieved at being alive than those who did not want to die. Conversely, those who wanted to die were most annoyed that they were still alive. The ambivalents and those who wanted to die were most likely to realize that they were putting their lives at risk. Not surprisingly, those who did not want to die were least aware of the risk of their actions. This has implications for prevention which we will address in Chapter 9. Finally, the ambivalents tended to perceive the parasuicide act as more aggressive than the other two groups.

Acts of non-fatal self-harm are commonly referred to as attempted suicide but they are treated both clinically and in research in a variety of ways (see Chapter 2). A majority of hospital-admitted non-fatal acts of self-injury are not usually defined as attempts at suicide in the strict sense. This is partly because psychiatric review may indicate that they have low suicide intent or little evidence of preparation and planning. However, in many cases people convey a sense of ambivalence about what they have done: wanting to both live and die at the same time. This is an established characteristic of suicidal thinking, but many of those who engage in self-harm appear to have poorly formulated intentions. As we noted earlier, to circumvent the problem of suicide intent the term 'parasuicide' has been used to refer to all non-fatal, deliberate acts of self-harm that appear to be similar to completed suicide. While averting the issue of intent runs the risk of reducing the meaningfulness of the term 'parasuicide', it also conveys the idea that the group embraced by this label is extremely heterogeneous.

There are relatively few studies of how people who attempt suicide communicate with others about what has happened and why. The psychological pain men and women experience prior to a parasuicide episode does not differ qualitatively. The association between depression and parasuicide is strong although many who attempt suicide are not clinically diagnosed with depression. Hence, it is important to include self-report when considering the contribution of depression. For example, people who describe themselves as being particularly depressed (but not diagnosed as such) may be at greater risk than someone who is clinically diagnosed and on a treatment protocol.

Interpersonal problems are frequently given as the reason for the depression that precipitated the suicide attempt. Many feel that their GP could or would not help when the presenting problem was affective rather than physical in nature. The importance of the link between physical health and depression was also observed.

Unbearable psychological pain and temporary relief from an intolerable situation are often offered as reasons for a suicide attempt. It seems that, for many, the episode is operant – to stop psychological pain temporarily or to highlight a current situation. In terms of prevention and intervention, it is the motivation behind the parasuicide episode and not the situational variable *per se* (e.g. interpersonal crisis) that is of importance and requires modification. These people see their suicidal act as the only behaviour which can (1) temporarily stop psychological pain or (2) highlight their current situation. They may have already tried other 'traditional' means of communication and coping but these have failed.

Having close friends in which to confide does not necessarily buffer against suicide. Many who attempt suicide say they have friends in whom they can confide and regard confiding in others as useful. However, the majority report feeling very alone. Thus, O'Connor et al. found that of those in their sample who were in a relationship at the time they attempted suicide, only one-third felt that their partner was helpful on occasions of need. These people are able to recognize how a partner or friend can be helpful in times of need but still feel lonely even when surrounded by friends.

Those who make repeated attempts at suicide express less remorse and are more angry and aggressive. Those who verbalize an intention to commit suicide are more likely to have a history of self-harm than those described as 'non-verbalizers' or 'ambivalents'. Those with an ambivalent attitude are more relieved at being alive than those who do not want to die. This may reflect their state of mind before the attempt. After the attempt they may have realized what they 'nearly did' and subsequently experience greater relief than those who did not want to die. Those who do not want to die (non-verbalizers) appear to be least aware of the life-threatening risk associated with their actions.

Conclusion

Those who engage in suicidal behaviour give a multitude of reasons as to why they engaged in such dangerous activities. Some admit suicidal intent, others do not and others still are ambivalent. An interpersonal crisis is a frequently cited precipitating negative life event. What is important, however, is not necessarily the actual life event or crisis, but the individual's view of the parasuicidal episode: do they view it as aggressive, are they angry or remorseful? These are the types of question we, as carers, should ask ourselves. Knowing the answers might help us avoid such situations arising again and may avert a suicide death in the future.

Chapter review

- In the days leading up to their attempt the parasuicidal person experiences a number of subtle changes in basic physiological activity such as sleep disturbance and changes in eating habits.
- Vacillations in mood and conflicting emotions are a feature of many suicide notes. They are also evident in emotional responses after a suicide attempt.
- Those who make repeated attempts at suicide tend to be less relieved at being alive than those who make a first attempt; they are also more angry, express less remorse, more fully appreciate the risk they took and are more likely to interpret their attempt as an act of aggression.
- Those who verbalize an intention to commit suicide are more likely to have a history of self-harm than those described as 'non-verbalizers' or 'ambivalents'.
- Those with an ambivalent attitude are more relieved at being alive than those who do not want to die.

8
Assisted Suicide

Discussions about suicide are often profoundly moral in character and nowhere is this more evident than when one person seeks help to hasten their own death. Psychologists and other users of talking, thinking and behaving therapies are normally spared the dilemmas presented to physicians who have at their disposal the means to end life painlessly. However, when a person pursues a serious conversation about the possibility of ending his or her own life they are, at the very least, exploring the advantages and disadvantages of suicide, clarifying their motives and intentions and perhaps seeking guidance on their best course of action. It is never easy for a person to ask another to talk through the suicide option. A direct request amounts to asking someone to assist in a serious criminal offence and some would regard that in itself as indicative of an 'unbalanced mind'. More usually requests are subtle or cryptic: 'I'm weary of it all.' 'I can't take much more of this.' 'Lucky Jane, she passed on last week.' These are not incidental utterances. To refuse to engage in a dialogue with someone making such statements could be harmful to the person and a serious breach of duty to act responsibly to protect them from impeding harm. On the other hand the effort made to engage in dialogue on the choosing of life or death could be construed as offering implicit approval of, and tacit reinforcement for, the suicide option.

In exploring the history of contemporary perspectives on suicide we concluded that, traditionally, mental health professionals tended to deny the concept of rational suicide and preferred to frame the anatomy of suicide within the psychology of the abnormal. Thus, rational suicide has often been regarded as an oxymoron: 'suicide must be either irrational or a product of mental illness' (Hendin, 1982). However, in recent years the possibility of rational suicide has gained wider recognition, partly due to the publicity surrounding patients' demands and partly due to the influence of the 'right-to-die' movement. Recent surveys suggest that the overwhelming majority of mental health professionals now believe that people can be capable of making rational, well-informed decisions about the timing and manner of their death (Werth and Liddle, 1994).

Notwithstanding this wider acceptance of rational suicide, many psychologists and other healthcare professionals question the motivation behind requests for assistance, especially when the person appears not to be terminally ill and the plea is made in the absence of demonstrable suffering. It is not that those seeking assistance are considered deranged, but that they are normally judged not to be receiving appropriate assistance with their pain or help in addressing their frequently unrealistic worries about family and financial matters and other resolvable psychosocial problems. A more insightful view points to the importance of going beyond manifest symptoms and the motives explicitly declared by the person, to exploring larger life circumstances, values, close relationships and philosophical or religious concerns. Without attempting to know a person at this deeper level, the activities of healthcare professionals can sometimes amount to technical interventions that ignore the person as a whole.

Jamison (1997) offers the following useful questions to help clarify your own views on assisted suicide:

- Do I think that a request for assisted suicide, whether explicit or implied, can ever be rational? If so, am I professionally capable of making such a determination?
- Is it appropriate for me to help a client die without the absolute certainty that the request is rational and voluntary? If not, how might I achieve the competence to make such a determination?
- Is assisted death merely another form of suicide? If so, is it appropriate or inappropriate for me to discuss the possibility of such an act with a client, given the complex risks?
- Is my refusal to discuss assisted death a form of abandonment?
- Is my willingness to talk through assisted suicide a form of intervention that actually increases the risk of suicide?

In answering each of these questions for ourselves we engage in a personal dialogue pervaded by ethical issues as well as emotional and practical concerns surrounding a response. These usually relate to the:

- personal autonomy and dignity of the person seeking assistance;
- quality of care we can offer;
- evidence available to help us interpret the request;
- distinction between enabling and allowing death;
- level of assistance we feel we can offer;
- value society places on individual lives;
- larger social and legal consequences of assisting.

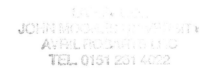

Personal autonomy

The ethical dilemmas posed in a request to assist with suicide are broadly equivalent to those encountered in debates on voluntary euthanasia. In the case of voluntary euthanasia the request is often particularly explicit and direct. The strongest arguments for assisted suicide are applied to circumstances where a person is:

1. terminally ill; and
2. unlikely to benefit from the discovery of a cure during what remains of his or her life; and
3. suffering unbearable pain or only capable of staying alive by enduring an intolerable dependence on medical technologies; and
4. communicating an abiding wish to die, as distinct from an impulsive request; and
5. seeking assistance voluntarily and rationally or has, prior to losing the competence to do so, expressed a wish to die in the event that circumstances 1–4 are satisfied; and
6. unable to commit suicide without the help of others.

Some advocates of assisted suicide take the view that these conditions are unduly restrictive. For example, they relate only to assisting suicide among those who are terminally ill and do not extend to victims permanently and profoundly incapacitated in, say, road traffic accidents.

The central ethical tenet for assisted suicide is based on the principle of personal autonomy and, by implication, the duty to respect the autonomy of others. People should be allowed to take the important decisions affecting their lives in accordance with their own view of how they want to live. In exercising autonomy people are empowered, and choices about the manner of dying and the timing of one's death should be part of what is involved in taking responsibility for one's life. Removing or curtailing these choices involves dis-empowering people because it diminishes their personal autonomy. Of course, the principle of personal autonomy does not require anyone asked to assist with suicide to comply nor in any way to act contrary to their personal moral or professional values.

Critics of assisted suicide point out that a terminally ill person is typically in a compromised and debilitated state, both physically and emotionally, and by definition is rarely truly competent to judge whether or not life is really worth living. Some, especially those in the hospice movement, argue that a request for assisted suicide is often motivated by an attempt to avoid the feared process of dying. Thus, a request may be motivated by a desire to escape from, typically unrealistic, fears about suffering or abandonment.

On a personal level, the question for a psychologist or other health-care worker is whether you can ethically support such a decision on the basis of the personal autonomy and plea for mercy from the person seeking your help. These principles provide a good starting point for assessing your own views and feelings about assisted suicide. Jamison (1997) offers the following questions:

- Do I regard assisted suicide as a form of killing?
- Can I justify assisted suicide on any grounds? If I can what are these grounds: personal autonomy, mercy or both?
- Is professional assistance with suicide ever really justified? If I think so, under what circumstances?
- Could it happen that I would regard the suffering of a client to be so severe as to justify an in-depth examination of the request for assisted suicide, to the point of supporting the person's decision to end his or her own life?
- Might the suffering of a client be so severe as to morally justify my giving assistance such as psychological support or other forms of encouragement?

Quality of care

Opponents of assisted suicide argue that modern medicine and palliative care mean that it is unnecessary for anyone to die while suffering from overwhelming pain. Thus, in talking through a request for help with suicide a healthcare practitioner will usually explore a range of options. However, while it is true that significant advances have been made in the management of pain and the provision of palliative care, not everyone will choose these alternatives, nor should they be compelled or cajoled to do so. Moreover, the alternatives are not a panacea and will often have consequences in terms of protracted illness, loss of awareness or diminished quality of life. One should also bear in mind that the pain endured by some who are terminally ill is not always caused by the illness itself. The suffering may be due to the way in which one's life has become defined by chemicals and machinery. In these circumstances the availability of auxiliary pain control methods may be at least irrelevant and possibly a factor in their request.

Insufficient evidence

Requests for assistance with suicide cannot be treated equally. Insight into motives will vary: some will be relatively clear about what they are asking but many will want to use talk about suicide to bring into consideration a complex web of personal, family and spiritual concerns. For some, talking about 'poor quality of life', and the prospect of 'things getting much worse' are the only ways to explore the massive personal loss being suffered. This raises questions about whether we can ever possess sufficient evidence to conclude that a person's request to be helped to die is insightful and genuinely voluntary.

The issue here is complicated by family dynamics. People do not live in a social vacuum and the quality of relationships with family members can often be a significant factor in a person's assessment of the suicide option. Some may feel alienated from their family – perhaps as a consequence of communication difficulties caused by their distress or illness; others may wish to relieve loved ones of a perceived burden of care. Mapping family dynamics is important for two reasons: first, to understand how family relationships may be shaping a person's thinking on suicide: a desire to keep one's wishes secret may in itself be indicative of family conflicts. Second, ethical issues arise concerning the propriety of disclosing a person's suicidal thoughts or plans to the family. Moreover, should family members come to hear of requests for help with suicide, their responses, which may range from acceptance to outright hostility, will come to play a significant part in the final outcome.

A moral argument against assisted suicide is that we can never possess sufficient information to conclude that a person is communicating a settled preference for death. Indeed some would argue that where a person's family indicates agreement with the wishes of someone seeking suicide there is prima facie evidence for thinking that the request may not be genuinely voluntary: coercion or subtle forms of external influence may be guiding the choice. Both supporters and critics of assisted suicide agree that any request should be followed by a period of reflection and dialogue, if only to discriminate between one-off, impulsive petitions and more enduring appeals. The more fundamental objection is that no one would ever rationally and voluntarily wish their own death, that such thinking is transitory and, given time and appropriate support, people will come round to choosing life. However, supporters argue that the premise of this argument begs its own conclusion by defining the option of suicide as intrinsically abnormal and needing correction.

Enabling or allowing death

Physicians are permitted to act in ways that will have negative consequences for their clients. They are allowed to do this when, for example, the medication they are administering will have damaging side-effects on a person's well-being but where the costs are considered not to outweigh the long-term benefit. Thus, according to the doctrine of 'double effect', it is permissible to alleviate pain by administering life-shortening drugs such as morphine. However, to assist suicide by giving a dose with the intention of shortly terminating a person's life is judged morally indefensible. According to this view assisted suicide constitutes active intervention to cause death by 'unnatural' means, whereas death caused by the side-effects of drugs or a person's wish to withdraw from a treatment programme reflects a more natural course. Opponents argue that the doctrine of double effect is irrelevant to decisions about assisted suicide because the doctrine applies only to circumstances where a person's death is harmful to his or her best interests. If a person considers imminent death *beneficial* rather than harmful, then the doctrine of double effect is irrelevant to the debate about the permissibility of the request.

Passive versus active assistance

Those who regard assisted suicide as morally wrong sometimes draw a distinction between passive and active assistance. The distinction is usually made with reference to passive euthanasia, which is often considered morally acceptable in certain circumstances. For example, a person who is terminally ill might be 'allowed to die' rather than linger through the relentless application of chemical and mechanical techniques. In withdrawing the treatment one is not intentionally killing the person, rather they die because of the unavoidable progress of the underlying disease. This is regarded as different from active euthanasia and directly assisted suicide because the latter requires a more deliberate act of killing. Closer consideration reveals the distinction is problematic (Kuhse, 1987). Whether assistance is considered in terms of acts of intervention or omission is largely a matter of practicality rather than principle. The difference might be illustrated, in the case of a terminally ill person, as one between:

- 'pulling the plug' on an oxygen machine keeping a dying patient alive and not replacing the tank when it runs out; or
- offering people the keys of their car believing they plan to kill themselves as opposed to leaving them to locate the keys themselves.

More fundamentally, active assistance is regarded as akin to killing and as such morally worse than simply letting someone die. However, even this distinction has been challenged (Winkler, 1995). Consider the case of a person suffering from motor neurone disease who is completely dependent on a mechanical respirator. She finds her condition intolerable, and persistently argues to be removed from the respirator so that she may die. In agreeing to the request is one simply letting the patient die? It doesn't seem plausible to regard the withdrawal of this life-sustaining measure as involving anything less than an intention to help terminate the person's life in line with her well-reasoned request.

Individual versus communal value of life

The principles of personal autonomy and self-determination underlie the moral argument for assisted suicide, but there are competing principles that drive a further counterargument. The ethical principles underlying an individual's decision to end his or her own life do not prescribe the basis on which public policy should be formulated. Communities have a right to value the lives of their members independently of the view any of them might have about the value of their own life. According to this argument, policy on assisted suicide should be formulated on shared social values and not exclusively on the personal autonomy of individuals. However, there are tensions here. At present the law does not allow people to consent to their own death, although the right to decide about receiving life-sustaining treatment is based on respect for a person's autonomy. In practice, the principle of individual self-determination is favoured in circumstances where the person chooses life, but problematic when they choose death. In much the same way, assisted suicide can be regarded as both affirming and contradicting acceptable ethical standards of professional practice. In theory, establishing suitable procedures for giving consent to assisted suicide should be no harder than establishing procedures for making an informed decision to refuse unwanted medical treatment. In practice, reluctance to decriminalize assisted suicide is probably motivated by concerns examined earlier in this chapter: namely, the difficulties thought to exist in establishing the genuineness of a request and any consent given.

The slippery slope

It is often said that if society were to decriminalize the giving of help to commit suicide it would place it on a morally slippery slope that would inevitably lead to, for example, non-voluntary euthanasia. It is certainly the case that offering assistance with suicide is an inherently social act – it cannot be thought of as an abstracted professional intervention. Thus, offering any form of assistance may lead to concerns that 'if I help in this way now, where might it all end?' At one level the concern here may be more illusory than real. There is nothing logically inconsistent in supporting voluntary euthanasia and assisted suicide while rejecting non-voluntary euthanasia, for example. Assisted suicide is based on clear principles, such as those described at the beginning of this chapter, that discriminate this kind of behaviour from acts of non-voluntary euthanasia. The strongest empirical evidence against the slippery slope argument comes from studies of the incidence of voluntary euthanasia in the Netherlands. Studies have repeatedly shown that physician-assisted deaths are based only on voluntary choices and agreements between individuals and the medical and legal authorities (van der Maas et al., 1991, 1996; van der Wal et al., 1992, 1996). Thus, there is no empirical evidence for frightening oneself into concluding that allowing assisted suicide under carefully defined circumstances will lead to moral decline into non-voluntary euthanasia or worse.

Although death is a certainty there is no guarantee that our deaths will be to our liking. At one time or another we are all concerned about what the last phase of our lives will be like. We may be worried that our dying might involve us in great suffering and wish to retain some dignity and control as life comes to an end. These concerns are warranted by choices we can make from among the technological innovations available for managing and extending the dying phase of our lives. Thinking through the available choices involves making decisions about the mix between self-determination and the quality of life we wish to have.

Those providing healthcare to others are regularly in contact with people who, at one time or another, may have considered taking their own lives. In most jurisdictions responding to a direct request by giving assistance involves crossing a criminal boundary. Such direct and explicit requests are relatively rare and pleas for assistance with the dying can often be subtle and indirect. The quality of a response to any request is guided by the quality, in terms of openness and clarity, of communication:

- people have with themselves as they exercise their personal autonomy and make important decisions about their own lives and death;
- within the respondents: how the healthcare workers talk through with themselves how they may respond;
- between the person seeking assistance and the healthcare worker;
- between the person seeking assistance, his or her family and the healthcare professional.

Conclusion

In addressing the ethical, emotional and practical concerns that pervade a serious dialogue on assisted suicide, Jamison (1997) offers healthcare professionals a range of guiding questions, including these:

- Have I comprehensively examined all the personal and professional risks that might be involved in helping a person take his or her own life?
- Have I fully considered how offering this help might affect me emotionally and in my dealings with others?
- Have I taken into account the rights, feelings and needs of the person's family?
- Have I fully examined the psychological risks to the family?
- Have I explained to the person that, as part of a healthcare team, I need to inform others of the request?
- Have I explored with the person a comprehensive range of alternatives to suicide?
- Am I treating my decision to offer assistance, directly or indirectly, as a last resort?

Fixed, rigid positions about whether it is right or wrong to assist with suicide are of little use. It is much more valuable to talk through, in an open and clear fashion, all the options as possible solutions.

Chapter review

- It is never easy for a person to ask another to talk through the suicide option.
- Traditionally, mental health professionals have denied the concept of rational suicide although in recent years the possibility of rational suicide has gained wider recognition.
- The central ethical tenet for assisted suicide is based on the principle of personal autonomy and, by implication, the duty to respect the autonomy of others.
- The ethical dilemmas posed in a request to assist with suicide are broadly equivalent to those encountered in debates on voluntary euthanasia.
- Fixed positions about whether it is right or wrong to assist with suicide are less valuable than talking through, in an open and clear fashion, all the options as possible solutions.

9

Suicide prevention

People attempt suicide for many reasons and, as we have seen, unfortunately many succeed. There is a multitude of explanations for why this is the case (as reviewed in the earlier chapters) as well as a plethora of precipitants and suicidal correlates. Hence all intervention or prevention strategies must represent and account for this heterogeneity. On personal, social and economic grounds we are all charged with reducing the incidence of this human tragedy. Therefore, if we are to go any way in reducing the suicide rate, substantial change is required – not simply change at the level of the individual psyche but root and branch change in society.

For example, young men in particular must be encouraged to avail themselves of the healthcare services. Some of them live and die the stress-weakness stigma. That is, they find themselves in stressful situations, employ inadequate coping strategies and become entangled in a vicious cycle of despair yet still they do not make use of the specialist services. What is it about these individuals specifically and society more generally that prevents them from seeking help? To answer this question we must focus on two generic types of prevention strategies: prevention strategies aimed at the individual and prevention strategies aimed at society. This chapter reviews current thinking from these two perspectives. The former is concerned with therapies, training and treatment for the individual. The latter addresses the wider context, those societal mechanisms that moderate the prevalence of suicide: for instance, reducing access to suicidal means and procedures that change our attitudes towards mental illness.

Access to means

Reducing access to lethal means can reduce suicide death. This has been shown over the years across different countries. In England and Wales there was a large fall in suicides for men and women in the 1960s and this is believed to be due to the substitution of natural gas for toxic coal gas which made suicide by gas almost impossible (Kreitman, 1976). As a result, by 1970 approximately 15 per cent of suicides were domestic gas poisonings and by 1990 death by this means had all but disappeared (see Chapter 2). Not surprisingly, the rates began to rise again as people chose alternative means of suicide such as carbon monoxide poisoning via car exhausts. Suicide by carbon monoxide poisoning has increased at the same time as motor vehicle use has increased. For this reason the fitting of catalytic converters (to reduce the toxicity of the exhaust fumes) and reshaping car exhausts (to make it more difficult to attach hoses) are central to national suicide prevention strategies.

Handguns

In the US, it has been shown that the availability of handguns, as measured by the strictness of gun control statutes across states, is associated with lower rates of suicide by handgun (Lester, 1989b). In those with stricter statutes there is also a preponderance of alternative methods of suicide but the overall suicide rate is still lower than in those with less stringent gun control laws. This is important; few people, when actively suicidal, are likely to change from their preferred means of suicide and kill themselves, if this method is unavailable. This is not to say that when they are not actively suicidal that they do not contemplate using another method. It may be that the alternative method is less lethal, therefore increasing the likelihood of interception and subsequent prevention. This suggests that countries experiencing high levels of suicide by handgun should review their gun licensing laws.

Overdosing on medication

In the UK, since September 1998, the size of packets of paracetamol sold in supermarkets and general shops has been reduced. The government has limited the number of tablets per packet to 16, with packets of a hundred being sold only to individuals suffering from chronic pain. Paracetamol packets also carry new health warnings to highlight the risks of ingesting analgesics. This is of great practical importance as many people who ingest tablets are not fully aware of the risk of their actions. Familiarity breeds complacency, in the sense that paracetamol tablets are so commonly available that often we do not think they could kill us – especially in doses of 20. The reality is that 20 paracetamol tablets taken with sufficient quantities of alcohol could result in death. Work that we have carried out has supported this notion. First-time parasuicides are often unaware of the risk of their actions and simply take the tablets because they are handy and easy to ingest (O'Connor et al., 2000). Hence, reducing the number of tablets available over-the-counter should limit access and availability. This ought to have a positive impact on the impulsive overdoses that are common among young people and also reduce unintentional suicides.

The introduction of more explicit health warnings on packaging should deter some of those who say that they did not want to die in the first place. This group is less likely to be aware of the risk of ingesting tablets and perhaps they would not do so if they recognized the dangers. These warnings will not enhance the attractiveness of the tablets to 'more serious' attempters who are likely to be already aware of the risks (see Chapter 8). Keith Hawton and colleagues, at Oxford, investigated the preventative effects of dispensing analgesics in blister packs. It was hoped that this new packaging would reduce their use in self-poisoning but this appeared to have little effect. Hawton et al. (1996) found that 60 per cent of self-poisoners still used tablets from the blister packs, albeit in smaller quantities. Based on the existing literature, Lewis and colleagues calculated population attributable fractions (PAF) which effectively, are indices of the impact of intervention strategies on the incidence of suicide (Lewis et al., 1997). They reviewed high-risk preventive strategies, for example interventions aimed at men and women recently discharged from psychiatric hospital and population-based strategies, like the reduction of availability of commonly used methods or the reduction of unemployment. Their conclusions were not as encouraging as they might have been, in particular when taken in the context of the UK government's desire to reduce the current suicide rate. With this in mind, it seems that reducing the availability of methods (e.g. introduction of blister packs and limiting packets of analgesics to 16) as well as trying to reduce the level of unemployment will be more effective than the other prevention strategies they reviewed.

Much of the work on suicide prevention is based on the accident prevention literature and is guided by three general principles:

1. to get people to change the behaviour that places them at risk;
2. to improve laws to reduce the opportunities for risk-taking behaviour;
3. to modify the environment.

In terms of suicide prevention, the first principle is concerned with encouraging people to avail themselves of healthcare services and not to abuse alcohol or drugs. Changing the law, thereby reducing access to lethal means, is a good example of the second principle. There are numerous instances of the third principle whereby the environment has been modified to reduce the risk from suicide: the substitution of natural gas for coal gas; the introduction of catalytic converters; the reshaping of exhaust pipes; the introduction of automatic doors on trains. Programmes concerned with managing suicidal individuals in prisons are based on such principles (see Chapter 4).

Suicide prevention in early psychosis

As outlined in Chapter 3, there is substantial risk of suicide in early psychosis. The Early Psychosis Prevention and Intervention Centre (EPPIC) in Melbourne, Australia has been designed specifically to reduce the incidence of young psychotic suicide. Since its inception in 1992 the centre has treated approximately 250 cases of psychosis annually and only ten people have committed suicide (McGorry et al., 1998). In itself, ten is too many, but this is a reduction compared to previous cohorts examined before the creation of the centre. McGorry and his colleagues offer guidelines for the development of prevention programmes for those with psychosis. Such programmes should aim:

1. to enhance the early detection of psychosis;
2. to improve mechanisms for access to psychiatric services;
3. to develop 'user-friendly' non-stigmatizing mental health services for young people;
4. to develop adequate supports for the carers of individuals with psychosis;
5. to develop more effective treatments for those with, or at risk of, developing early psychosis;
6. to establish suicide prevention structures within health services (McGorry et al., 1998).

In the main, these basic principles can be applied to prevent all types of suicide. For instance, they highlight the importance of developing a user-friendly and non-stigmatizing healthcare system. In Britain and Ireland this is especially pertinent. Young men, in general, still feel the stigma of presenting with psychological disorders to healthcare professionals. Their response to this stigma is non-participation, in that they do not present to their GP as they are ashamed: they regard a public admission of this type of problem as a weakness (O'Connor et al., 2000). Unfortunately, the stereotypes of 'tough' men, 'men don't cry' persist: 'there is still a significant public stigma associated with psychological disorders, and many people still feel that to be categorized as having a psychological problem reflects a lack of moral fibre or spinelessness in themselves' (Priest, 1991).

The early diagnosis of depression is now a central tenet of GP training. To this end, the Defeat Depression campaign (Priest, 1994) was launched in association with the Royal College of Psychiatrists and the Royal College of General Practitioners to raise awareness of affective illness among GPs and the general public. Essentially its purpose is to assess GPs' ability to diagnose depressive illness and to reduce the stigma associated with affective disorders in general. It has been estimated that one in 20 adults suffers from depression at any given time, and that 70 per cent of these cases go untreated (Kelly and France, 1987).

Further research must address the underlying reasons that continually prevent many men from availing themselves of the primary heathcare services. GPs ought to be trained better in the identification of suicidal individuals, and men must be encouraged to contact their GPs in times of distress. This is a difficult task but the economic benefits are huge – parasuicidal behaviour costs the National Health Service hundreds of thousands of pounds per annum.

Prevention and education strategies

Potential suicides come in many different guises and, as outlined previously, healthcare professionals are often unaware of the degree of diversity within the suicidal population. For example, suicidal individuals frequently do not present with the traditional risk factors; therefore they remain untreated and, unfortunately, a small proportion go on to end their lives. It is not surprising, therefore, that experiences such as these engender feelings of inadequacy among healthcare professionals. Some professionals are unaware of the changing face of suicide. This must be rectified.

Many GPs believe wrongly that 'talking about suicide' increases the likelihood of a patient actually attempting suicide (Shneidman, 1985). This may be because GPs encounter more psychiatric-type suicides and this may lead them to overestimate the prevalence of this particular type of suicide. Traditionally, it has been the view that only individuals with a history of psychiatric illnness kill themselves. This is not the case. A recent study of ours has shown that the traditional picture of suicide may only be true 15 per cent of the time, the remainder are atypical – they are 'normal' people (O'Connor et al., 1999b). Thus GPs may not know, for example, that enquiring about suicidal thoughts is an accurate method of risk assessment that does not induce risk from suicide.

The very nature of this complex problem demands wide ranging education and prevention strategies that encompass the needs of all concerned: the suicidal person, the healthcare professional and the general public. Educating the public at large will yield two outcomes: the general public will become more aware of the risk factors and secondly they may change their attitudes towards suicide.

We propose five general education and prevention strategies aimed at these three groups (high-risk individuals, healthcare professionals and the general public).

Communication

The importance of communication ought to be promoted, and men in particular should be encouraged to communicate their worries and anxieties. This strategy can be implemented in many ways and at different levels. Recent research suggests that at-risk individuals have difficulty communicating with others, in particular when they are experiencing interpersonal problems. As a result, in some countries children are taught from an early age about the importance of effective skills.

Coping strategies

The coping strategies of suicidal individuals must be dysfunctional, in some way, if they lead people to perceive suicide as the only option. Research into coping strategies should help identify differences in suicidal and non-suicidal individuals' coping abilities. Proactive coping should form part of education packages, and these coping strategies should draw on communication (and vice versa) and be aimed at children and young people. Other forms of coping strategies ought to be considered, including seeking social support and religious coping (turning to one's religion for comfort in difficult times). In particular, it is known that religious coping can buffer against suicide.

Other interpersonal problems need to be addressed. For instance it is evident from suicide notes and interviews with parasuicides that many people perceive the suicide (attempt) as aggressive, either directed at themselves or others. We need to investigate the psychological correlates of aggression in this situation. Why do some people perceive the suicidal act as aggressive and others not? Could personality variables predict the aggressive suicide?

Destigmatization of stressors

Suicidal people often regard an inability to cope with a stressful situation as a personal weakness. It is not. It is necessary both to change the general perceptions of stressors and also to determine whether people are misinterpreting their personal situations. In other words, to what extent do they perceive their situation in a cognitively rigid and distorted fashion? Here again, communication with significant others and healthcare professionals is beneficial. It is essential that the psychological impact of stressful life events on the individual is assessed. Many issues remain unresolved: for example, is there a suicide-mediating type of stressor? We know that the occurrence of a stressful life event is only indirectly associated with suicide risk; it is our perceptions of the stressful life events that are crucial to the prediction of suicide.

Destigmatization of affective disorders and knowledge of suicidal risk factors

The prevalence of depression must be highlighted. Members of the general public are often surprised at how many people actually suffer from depression at least once in their lives. While perceptions of depression and the other affective disorders have changed significantly in recent years (Michel and Valach, 1992) there remains still a need to destigmatize depression and anxiety. Suffering from depression, lowered affect or anxiety is not abnormal. Moreover, anyone of us could be at risk from suicide.

Awareness of existing services

Many people are unaware of the services that are available for counselling and helping individuals cope with affective illness. Counselling services should be used more often in conjunction with GP consultations. Others who know of the existence of such services may not want to use them because of the associated stigma. The stigma associated with the 'helping services' has to be reduced. One step would be to encourage young people to telephone the specialist helplines in times of distress.

Why do they not talk about their problems or seek help?

These people (usually men) have been socialized so as to value coping strategies based on keeping problems self-contained, private and self-managed. There is evidence to support this view. Some individuals have support mechanisms in place but do not use them adequately. For instance, many parasuicides confide in their friends and family and still feel alone. One would not expect people who had close friends to confide in to report feeling lonely. That they do, suggests that their coping strategies differ from those who are not suicidal; these differences, however, have yet to be determined.

Types of social support

Further research is needed to gain a better understanding of the relationship between the quantity and quality of social support, to help us recognize low levels of social support. We must distinguish between intimate and casual social support. Usually, employment guarantees some level of social support provided by colleagues, but it seems that these support networks are not adequate to prevent suicide. The enhancement of coping strategies should include promoting the use of social networks as support mechanisms. In sum, global interventions are required involving:

- destigmatization of affective disorders;
- increasing awareness of and accessibility to available services.

It is important that the Samaritans and other counselling services are promoted and presented in a more accessible manner. Employers should employ counsellors to run training programmes aimed at stress management and emotion expression. One of the psychosocial factors implicated in the rising trend in male suicide death is the inability to cope with a changing social role. A 'macho' manner of stress management is placing individuals at higher risk.

The Samaritans and suicide prevention centres

The Samaritans, founded in 1953 by Chad Varah, now receives over 4.5 million calls a year, from callers in the UK and Ireland, at over 200 branches. All volunteers are governed by seven principles and seven practices. These include: to be available at any hour of the day or night, to alleviate human misery, to be completely confidential and not to impose their own beliefs and convictions on callers. Without doubt, the thousands of volunteers do an outstanding job in alleviating callers' misery and, in some cases, preventing suicide. However, it is difficult to determine how effective this service is in terms of long-term suicide prevention. There is no easy way to determine, empirically, how effective it is, or how it could be improved to enhance its efficacy. If we measure the frequency of use of a service as a crude measure of its need, then indeed, there is an enormous need for the Samaritans – hence their work must continue and expand.

Another prevention organization, not yet in vogue in the UK and Ireland, is the Suicide Prevention Center. All across the United States and further afield, suicide prevention centres exist to provide physical as well as telephone support for the suicidal. Essentially, these are crisis-intervention centres and have existed since the 1950s. It may be that people in the UK and Ireland are too reserved, or inhibited by the fear of stigmatization, to use such centres and, as a result, on the whole, they do not exist. This possibility underlines further the need to destigmatize all mental disorders, stress and coping strategies as well as suicidal behaviour. The setting up of crisis-intervention centres ought to be central to national suicide prevention programmes. Year on year, governments set suicide targets, proclaiming a desire for a reduction in suicide. These may be honourable declarations and targets, but what is being done on the ground to bring about such reductions? In short, not enough. The establishment of crisis-intervention centres, in a suitably progressive and supportive environment, would certainly help bring the case of mental–psychological health into everyday parlance and acceptance. If we can lift the stigma, we can encourage others to participate, to avail themselves of existing services, to help them to help themselves.

The perception of suicidal behaviour and prevention

Since our perception of suicidal behaviour plays an important part in prevention, it is not helpful to consider such behaviour as abnormal. This view is wrong and maintains the associated stigma and taboo. Suicide and parasuicide are the result of an accumulation of complex precipitants that push someone 'over the edge'. The task of suicide prevention is not single-tracked. The dissemination of information on risk factors needs to be multi-tiered: aimed at the general public, mental health professionals and the at-risk individuals themselves. Specialist knowledge aids understanding which, in turn, aids prediction and subsequently prevention.

Care must be taken with the dissemination of information in television programmes, because the portrayal of suicide in the media is known to cause suicide clustering – suicides being clumped temporally and geographically in unusual ways (see, e.g., Gould, 1990). Glamourizing the suicides of public figures can trigger spates of copycat suicides (e.g. the suicide of Kurt Cobain, lead singer with the rock band Nirvana). The effects of portraying suicidal behaviour in the popular media are well reported but have yielded inconsistent results.

Here, we report on two famous self-poisonings shown on popular British television programmes: the soap opera *Eastenders* and the hospital drama *Casualty*. The case of *Eastenders* is often referred to as the 'Angie Effect'. In the soap, Angie, one of the programme's best loved stars, took an overdose after an interpersonal crisis – her husband was unfaithful. The episode was watched by many millions (an estimated

14 million on first showing), and subsequent studies reported that there was an increase in 'copy-cat' self-poisonings admitted to acute hospitals, presenting with a similar overdose (Ellis and Walsh, 1986). The evidence is disputed, however, and some researchers have concluded that the case for 'modelling' is not yet proven (e.g. Platt, 1987), saying that there was a rising trend before the episode anyway, or that adequate controls were not employed to draw firm conclusions.

More recently, the television drama *Casualty* made the headlines. The plot was somewhat similar to that in *Eastenders*, a fictional portrayal of a paracetamol overdose. On this occasion, the protagonist was an RAF pilot suffering from guilt after the accidental crash of the aircraft he was flying, killing a colleague. Hawton and colleagues investigated the impact of this episode on subsequent self-poisonings. They collected incidence data from 49 accident and emergency departments and psychiatric services in the UK (Hawton et al., 1999). Statistical analysis suggested that the presentations for self-poisoning increased by 17 per cent in the week following the telecast and by 9 per cent in the second week. More interesting, and yielding more support for the 'modelling' hypothesis, was that the increase in paracetamol poisoning was greater than that of non-paracetamol self-poisoning. Furthermore, of 32 patients interviewed, 20 per cent said that watching the episode had influenced their decision to take an overdose.

Taking both studies together, it is probably safe to conclude that care ought to be taken when broadcasters and the media, in general, decide to screen such programmes. Intuitively, we believe that the irresponsible coverage of these events can enhance the appeal of suicidal behaviour. The scientific research is not conclusive, but in such an area of study it is difficult to demonstrate the modelling effect with 100 per cent clarity. To take an everyday example, we are well aware of the importance of role models, and we know that social learning occurs. In the case of suicidal behaviour, for a person 'at risk' – contemplating self-harm – viewing a programme that glamourizes or legitimizes self-poisoning may make him or her more likely to engage in the act. To this end, Hawton and others argue that, if a suicide attempt is to be shown, it is important not to portray the method of overdose. They reason that it is more dangerous when we actually show a possible means (of suicide), by which a potentially suicidal person can translate his or her thoughts into actions (see Rogers and Carney (1994) and Platt (1993) for a discussion of the modelling effect).

If we accept that television does have an effect on suicidal behaviour, then we should harness this, transforming it from a precipitant to a preventative medium. As yet, the possibilities for prevention have not been fully explored. Currently, it is used only for projecting information to people: for example, the contact addresses for befriending organizations like the Samaritans. More than likely, with the dawn of the 21st century and the seemingly exponential growth of cable and satellite channels, television will begin to play a more proactive role in the prevention of suicidal behaviour – albeit employed with caution and common sense.

Recognizing risk

Previous research has shown that GPs often do not recognize patients at risk of suicide (Michel, 1986) and that they can be ignorant of the known correlates and precipitants (Rockwell and O'Brien, 1973). Caregivers' attitudes and knowledge also are thought to be important in suicide prevention (Kreitman, 1986). Michel and Valach (1992) tested this notion directly: they trained GPs in aspects of suicide prevention, focusing on their knowledge and attitudes towards suicide. They employed two methods of training and found that seminar-based training, not written material presented alone, improved the GPs' knowledge and attitudes towards suicide.

In addition, a Swedish study carried out postgraduate training with GPs on the island of Gotland, which has a population of 56,000 (Rutz et al., 1989, 1992), one psychiatric department and 18 GPs. In 1983 and 1984 the Swedish Prevention and Treatment of Depression Committee organized two education programmes aimed at identifying and treating depressive disorders. They monitored the suicide rates for the years 1982–1985 also, and reported a significant but temporary decrease after the education programmes. Rutz and colleagues argued that the decrease was only temporary because the effects of education had subsided. Although these results are promising, there have been several criticisms of the study, some of which went so far as to say that the published results are misleading. Nevertheless, this type of study warrants further investigation so that the effectiveness of such education programmes can be determined. This is one of the major challenges facing suicidologists, since, in the main, intervention and prevention strategies have not yet been properly investigated (see Gunnell and Frankel, 1994 for a review).

Can GPs prevent suicide?

A debate related to the Gotland study is whether or not GPs can prevent suicide. There is still no consensus as to whether GPs can predict and prevent suicide, irrespective of their knowledge of suicide risk factors. Despite the encouraging studies suggesting that upwards of 60 per cent of people visit their GP in the weeks or months before suicide, at least two fundamental questions require answers. First, are suicidal people more likely than members of the general population to visit their GP, when matched for age and gender? Second, are men, who represent the largest risk group, presenting to their GPs in the period before their death?

To answer the first question, a study in Scotland compared the GP attendance of those who committed suicide to a control group matched for age and sex (Power et al., 1997). This study yielded mixed results. Over the ten-year period of study, suicide patients attended their GP more frequently than the matched controls but in the month before their deaths there was no difference. However, when the suicides were examined in terms of whether or not they had a psychiatric history, the results were more promising. The GPs were more likely to have given the suicide cases a psychiatric diagnosis in comparison to the controls. This suggests that the GPs were identifying the associated mental disorders but, unfortunately, were unable to avert the suicide itself. It would seem, therefore, that while the GPs are identifying the predictors of suicide, these predictors are not sensitive enough to distinguish the suicidal from those who are not.

The second question concerns whether young men visit their GP shortly before death. If they do not, then any intervention aimed at the level of primary healthcare is fruitless. Unfortunately, in the current climate, men in general are not presenting to their GPs. In a study that we carried out in Northern Ireland of 142 suicides, the majority of males were thought to be depressed (not necessarily clinically diagnosed) and under stress, yet they still did not present to their GP in the six months before death (O'Connor et al., 1999b). One explanation for these low levels of attendance concerns the stigma attached to seeking medical assistance for a psychological problem. Another explanation relates to the lack of clarity of the role of a GP. As mentioned previously, many people are unaware that a GP can help, or advise, in such situations. We need concerted national campaigns to reverse this. These cannot be campaigns focused on suicide *per se* but on the precipitants of suicide and affective disorders. This has obvious resource implications; GPs are overworked as it is. However, if more at risk individuals present to their GPs, these people may be less likely to attempt suicide, thereby reducing the economic burden on other areas of the National Health Service such as Accident and Emergency departments.

In two recent studies, one in Northern Ireland, the other in Avon, England, there is evidence for a pattern of contact with healthcare professionals among suicides. In the Northern Irish sample (Foster et al., 1997), the time-lag between the last contact with a healthcare worker and death was greater among suicides aged under 30 (and male suicides generally are). A lifetime history of contact with mental health professionals was more common among older than younger suicides. Similarly in Avon (Vassilas and Morgan, 1997), the younger suicides were less likely to have contacted their GPs in the last year of their life, compared to the older suicides. These findings are not insignificant; we have to develop strategies so that potential young suicides go to their GPs and make contact with the health services, thus averting the meaningless waste of so many young lives.

Predicting suicide

The ability to prevent suicide is intertwined with the notion of prediction since it is extremely difficult to prevent a behaviour that we are unable to predict. But that is precisely what we are expecting GPs and other healthcare professionals to do. Prediction of suicide is so difficult because, in statistical terms, suicide is a rare event, and like other rare events it is very difficult to identify the who (who will attempt suicide) and the when (when they will make their attempts). Remember that to commit suicide you must first attempt suicide, so, effectively, clinicians are also trying to predict attempted suicide.

How can we predict which day will be the one when we actually die? In terms of prediction, we try to find the balance between sensitivity and specificity. Sensitivity can be said to be high if we correctly predict suicide and that person goes on to commit suicide (true positive), relative to the total number of suicides, whereas specificity is when we predict that there will be no suicide, and no suicide occurs, relative to the total number of people who do not commit suicide[1]. Pokorny (1993, 1983), in a landmark study, followed 4,800 psychiatric patients over a five-year period. In this time 67 of the patients committed suicide. He had made predictions about which of these individuals would and would not kill themselves. Table 9.1 illustrates how effective he was in predicting suicide among these 4,800 patients. Unsurprisingly, he was most effective in predicting that someone would not (and did not) commit suicide during the period of the study. However, this study only predicted suicide correctly in 55 per cent of the cases (true positives). This illustrates that suicide is difficult to predict with any accuracy, and in the 1993 follow-up study the prediction was no more impressive.

Suicide prevention and the Internet

The seemingly exponential growth of suicide, among the young in particular, has been matched by a similar growth in access and usage

---

1. The correct definition of sensitivity is: true positives divided by the sum of true positives and false negatives, multiplied by 100. Specificity is: true negatives divided by the sum of false positives and true negatives, multiplied by 100.

Table 9.1 Predicting suicide

Prediction	Outcome	
Predicted suicide	Suicide (55%)	No suicide (30 %)
	True positives	False positives
Predicted No Suicide	Suicide (44%)	No suicide (74 %)
	False negatives	True negatives

Source: Pokorny (1983, 1993)

of the Internet among young people throughout the world. We are already at the stage where university students are entitled to free Internet access, schools are developing information technology programmes and some Internet Service Providers are offering free Internet access. It is not surprising, therefore, that the Internet represents an invaluable means of communicating with and helping the very people who are killing themselves. It is an ideal medium through which to provide suicide prevention strategies and campaigns as there is relatively no stigma associated with email or 'surfing the net', and communication can be anonymous as well as interactive.

In this vein, several specialist suicide-related mailing lists have been set up to help those who are suicidal and those who encounter suicide, including researchers, carers and the bereaved. Mailing lists are similar to email: they provide a forum where a group of people can hold discussions. If there is a question that you would like to ask, simply post it electronically on the mailing list and anyone on the list is free to respond to your query or comment. There are three mailing lists with which we have had experience: (1) The Suicide-Prevention Mailing List; (2) The Suicide-Support Mailing List; and (3) The Suicide-Survivors Mailing List. Each of these mailing lists has different aims and membership as suggested by their names. For example, the suicide-support list provides support for individuals who are feeling suicidal; contributors to this list benefit from non-judgemental emotional support provided in a neutral environment. The Internet also provides a medium for the dissemination of recent research findings and frequently asked questions (FAQs) about suicide. There is a multitude of information available, some authorized by suicide prevention organizations, where people can go to obtain more information about suicide risk. Readers are directed to Stoney (1998) for further details.

There are drawbacks with using the Internet as a counselling tool, not to mention the ethical and social considerations. Do we want to foster a society that promotes counselling via email, or one where interpersonal problems are resolved across a computer terminal? These are concerns for the 21st century that require careful thought and scientific investigation. For the time being, however, the Internet is providing a means of support and dissemination that, as far as we know, benefits the individual.

Developing therapies for prevention

In Chapters 3 to 5 we described the characteristics of suicide and para-suicide. In particular in Chapter 5 we reported specific psychological characteristics that are thought to precipitate a suicide attempt: negative attributional style, problem-solving deficits, lack of future thinking, over-general memories and so on. In recent years, psychologists and others have developed treatment intervention programmes aimed at changing our ways of thinking so that we adopt less negative attributional styles or that train us in using more divergent strategies in problem-solving, so that when faced with life stresses and strains we are better able to cope and do not consider suicide as an option.

Problem-solving therapy

Problem-solving therapy is important because it is based on the assumption that irrespective of the aetiology of your situation, the suicide attempt is a communication of problem-solving failure of some kind or another. There are various frameworks favoured by different therapists and psychologists, but they are all guided by similar principles and structures. Hawton and Kirk (1989) endorse the following strategies:

- to identify the client's (or patient's) problems;
- to identify the client's resources;
- to obtain information from other sources (people and records);
- to decide whether the problem-solving therapy is feasible or appropriate;
- to decide on practical arrangements;
- to develop the therapeutic relationship.

Problem-solving techniques may not be suitable for everyone. After assessment, the clinician may decide to employ an alternative, adopting a variety of cognitive and behavioural techniques. The reader is directed to Mark Williams' handbook *The Psychological Treatment of Depression* (1996b) where he describes the psychological models of depression as well as assessment and treatment techniques which may be helpful when dealing with suicidal individuals. In the US, Marsha Linehan has pioneered Dialectical Behaviour Therapy (DBT), where she has combined individual therapy with group therapy sessions. As the name suggests she focuses on the expression of ideas, empathy and reflection, and employs a range of techniques drawn from behavioural, cognitive and psychotherapeutic backgrounds. Recent studies suggest that DBT yields longer term as well as immediate gains (Linehan et al., 1993). In one study (Linehan et al., 1993), the results show that the rates of parasuicidal behaviour among the DBT group were significantly lower than the control group.

Manual-assisted cognitive-behaviour therapy (MACT; Evans et al., 1999)

The MACT approach combines the principles of DBT, cognitive-behaviour therapy linked to problem-solving (Salkovskis et al., 1990) and cognitive therapy for antisocial and borderline personality disorder (Davidson and Tyrer, 1996). The aim of the MACT approach is to deliver a brief intervention, which may range from patients being given six booklets or manuals to receiving six sessions of cognitive-behaviour therapy. The authors of this programme reason, if parasuicide patients are given the six booklets and do not return for therapy, that this may be an intervention in itself. A randomized controlled trial has already been piloted using this procedure (Evans et al., 1999) and the results are encouraging. Patients presenting to two centres in west London, after an episode of deliberate self-harm, with personality disturbance and a history of self-harm in the previous 12 months, were considered for inclusion in the study. The treatment itself is between two and six sessions, organized around a manual of six short chapters (see Table 9.2), and is cognitively orientated and problem-focused. Initial results suggest that this type of intervention may indeed be beneficial in terms of reducing the levels of personal distress and the burden on the health service. At follow-up, six months later, those who were in the MACT treatment group had lower rates of suicidal acts per month and reduced depressive symptoms.

Table 9.2 Contents of the MACT manual

Chapter	Contents
1	Multiple case stories. Behavioural chain analysis of specific circumstances of recent episode of DSH. Advantages and disadvantages of DSH. Problem list.
2	Problem-solving techniques with worked case examples.
3	Self-monitoring of thoughts and feelings.
4	Distress coping strategies.
5	Education about dangers of alcohol and drug misuse. Strategies for reducing alcohol intake.
6	DSH attempt revisited. Skills deficit identified. Coping strategies for future identified.

Source: Evans et al. (1999).

Although the sample size was small, this study has formed the foundation for a larger, patient-centred manual-assisted project, conducted in multiple centres and funded by the Medical Research Council. This seems to be a sensible approach to the suicidal behaviour problem, finding a balance between patient care and patient autonomy. It will be particularly beneficial if it yields considerable results while keeping resources to a minimum. This may sound callous, but successful implementation of any solutions, in the longer term, have to be economically viable.

Conclusion

There are a variety of treatment interventions that reduce the incidence of parasuicidal behaviour and others that seem to be beneficial for tackling the precipitants of suicide. But these techniques need to be accompanied by societal change, so that people are encouraged to avail themselves of such treatments and enjoy the benefits. This slim volume has described how suicide is the result of a multitude of risk factors – psychological, social and clinical – and that there is no single pathway to suicide. We are still a long way from understanding fully why people kill themselves, but it is important to bear in mind that suicidal behaviour is not abnormal. The sooner suicidal behaviour becomes firmly rooted in the psychology of everyday life, the better equipped we will be, as individuals and as a society, to understand, and identify those at risk and perhaps even to prevent suicide.

Chapter review

- Prevention strategies should be at least twofold: aimed at the individual and aimed at society.
- Reducing access to lethal means can reduce suicide death.
- Mental health, stress and coping have to be 'normalized '– destigmatized.
- The role of GPs and healthcare professionals requires definition.
- Five general education and prevention strategies aimed at: high-risk individuals, healthcare professionals and the general public are suggested.
- Care must be taken if suicidal behaviour is portrayed in the media.
- More research is required to enhance our ability to recognize risk.
- Prevention and education strategies, utilizing modern technologies (e.g. the Internet) must be explored and evaluated.
- Individual, psychologically based therapies need further development and expansion.

References

Abramson, L.Y., Alloy, L.B. et al. (1998) Suicidality and cognitive vulnerability to depression among college students: A prospective study. *Journal of Adolescence, 21*, 473–487.

Allebeck, P. and Allgulander, C. (1990) Psychiatric diagnosis as predictors of suicide: A comparison of diagnoses at conscription and in psychiatric care in a cohort of 50,465 young men. *British Journal of Psychiatry 157*, 339–344.

Allport, G. (1942) *The Use of Personal Documents in Psychological Science*. New York: Social Science Research Council.

Alvarez, A. (1971) *Savage God*. London: Penguin.

Appleby, L. and Warner, R. (1993) Parasuicide: Features of repetition and the implications for intervention. *Psychological Medicine, 23*, 13–16.

Aquinas, St Thomas (1929) *Summa Theologica*. London: Burns, Oates and Washbourne.

Bancroft, J., Skrimshire, A., Casson, J., Harvard-Watts, O. and Reynolds, F. (1977) People who deliberately poison or injure themselves: Their problems and their contacts with helping agencies. *Psychological Medicine, 7*, 289–303.

Barraclough, B. (1971) Suicide in the elderly. In D. Kay and A. Walks (Eds) *Recent Developments in Psychogeriatrics*. Headly, Ashford, Kent: Royal Medico-Psychological Association.

Barraclough, B. (1987) *Suicide: Clincial and Epidemiological*. Croom Helm: New York.

Barraclough, B., Bunch, I., Nelson, B. and Sainsbury, P. (1974) A hundred cases of suicide: Clinical aspects. *British Journal of Psychiatry, 125*, 355–373.

Barraclough, B. and Pallis, D. (1975) Depression followed by suicide: a comparison of depressed suicides with living depressives. *Psychological Medicine, 5*, 55–61.

Baume, P. and McTaggart, P. (1998) Suicides in Australia. In R.J. Kosky, H.S Eshkevari, R.D. Goldney and R. Hassan (Eds) *Suicide Prevention: The Global Context*. New York: Plenum Press.

Baumeister, R.F. (1990) Suicide as escape from self. *Psychological Review, 99*, 90–113.

Beck, A.T. (1976) *Cognitive Therapy and the Emotional Disorders*. New York: International Universities Press.

Beck, A.T. and Steer, R.A. (1989) Clinical predictors of eventual suicide: A 5- to 10-year prospective study of suicide attempters. *Journal of Affective Disorders, 17*, 203–209.

Beck, A.T., Weissman, A., Lester, D. and Trexler, L. (1974) The measurement of pessimism: the hopelessness scale. *Journal of Consulting and Clinical Psychology, 42*, 861–865.

Berglund, M. (1984) Suicide in alcoholism – a prospective study of 88 suicides. 1 The multidimensional diagnosis at 1st admission. *Archives of General Psychiatry*, *41*, 888–891.

Bille-Brahe, U. and Jessen, G. (1994) Repeated suicidal behaviour: a two year follow-up. *Crisis, 15*, 77–82.

Bille-Brahe, U., Kerkhof, A., DeLeo, D., Schmidtke, A., Crepet, P., Lonnqvist, J., Michel, K., Salander-Renberg, E., Stiles, T.C., Wasserman, D., Aagaard, B., Egebo, H. and Jensen, B. (1997) A repetition–prediction study of European parasuicide populations: A summary of the first report from Part II of the WHO/EURO Multicentre Study on Parasuicide in cooperation with the EC Concerted Action on Attempted Suicide. *Acta Psychiatrica Scandinavica, 95*, 81–86.

Bille-Brahe, U. and Schmidtke, A. (1994) WHO/EURO: Multicentre study on parasuicide: development and progress. In M.J. Kelleher (Ed.) *Divergent Perspectives on Suicidal Behaviour*. Fifth European Symposium on Suicide. Cork: O'Leary Ltd.

Bjerg, K. (1967) The suicidal life space: Attempts at a reconstruction from suicide notes. In E. Shneidman (Ed.) *Essays in Self-destruction*. New York: Science House, Inc.

Black, D.W. and Winokur, G. (1990) Suicide and psychiatric diagnosis. In: S.J.Blumenthal and D.J. Kupfer (Eds) *Suicide Over the Life Cycle: Risk Factors, Assessment and Treatment of Suicidal Patients*. Washington, DC: American Psychiatric Press.

Black, D.W., Winokur, G. and Nasrallah, A. (1987) Treatment and outcome in secondary depression – a naturalistic study of 1087 patients. *Journal of Clinical Psychiatry, 48*, 438–441.

Black, S.T. (1993) Comparing genuine and simulated suicide notes: a new perspective. *Journal of Consulting and Clinical Psychology, 614*, 699–702.

Bleuler, E. (1950) *Dementia Praecox, or the Groups of Schizophrenia*. New York: International Universities Press.

Blumenthal, S. (1990) Youth suicide: risk factors, assessment, and treatment of adolescent and young adult suicidal patients. *Psychiatric Clinics of Northern America, 13* , 511–566.

Brent, D.A., Perper, J.A., Moritz, G., Allman, C., Friend, A., Roth, C., Schweers, J., Balach, L. and Baugher, M. (1993) Psychiatric risk factors for adolescent suicide: A case-control study. *Journal of the American Academy of Adolescent Psychiatry, 32*, 521–529.

Buda, M. and Tsuang, M.T. (1990) The epidemiology of suicide: Implications for clinical practice. In S.J. Blumenthal and D.J. Kupfer (Eds) *Suicide over the Life Cycle: Risk Factors, Assessment and Treatment of Suicidal Patients*. Washington DC: American Psychiatric Press.

Buglass, D. and Horton, J. (1974) A scale for predicting suicidal behaviour. *British Journal of Psychiatry, 124*, 573–578.

Bukstein, O.G., Brent, D.A., Perper, J.A., Moritz, G., Baugher, M., Schweers, J., Roth, C. and Balach, L. (1993) Risk factors for completed suicide among adolescents with a lifetime history of substance abuse: A case-control study. *Acta Psychiatrica Scandinavica, 88,* 403–408.

Bunch, J. (1972) Recent bereavement in relation to suicide. *Journal of Psychosomatic Research, 16,* 361–366.

Burtch, B.E. and Ericson, R.V. (1979) *The Silent System.* Toronto: University of Toronto Press.

Burvill, P.W. (1998) Migrant suicide rates in Australia and in country of birth. *Psychological Medicine, 28 ,* 201–208.

Camus, A. (1985) *The Myth of Sisyphus.* Harmondsworth: Penguin.

Capstick, A. (1960) Recognition of emotional disturbance and the prevention of suicide. *British Medical Journal, 1,* 1179–1182.

Carlson, G.A., Rich, C.L., Grayson, P. and Fowler, R.C. (1991) Secular trends in the psychiatric diagnoses of suicide victims. *Journal of Affective Disorders, 21,* 127–132.

Carnap, R. (1959) Psychology in physical language. In A. J. Ayer (Ed.) *Logical Positivism.* New York: Free Press. (original work published 1931)

Casper, J.L. (1825) *Beitrage zur medizinischen Statistik und Staatsarzeikunde.* Berlin: Drummler

Cattell, H.R. (1988) Elderly suicide in London: An analysis of coroners' inquests. *International Journal of Geriatric Psychiatry, 3,* 251–261.

Cattell, H. and Jolley, D.J. (1995) One hundred cases of suicide in elderly people. *British Journal of Psychiatry, 166,* 451–457.

Charlton, J., Kelly, S., Dunnell, K., Evans, B. and Jenkins, R. (1993) Suicide deaths in England and Wales: Trends in factors associated with suicide deaths. *Population Trends, 71,* 34–42.

Clarke-Finnegan, M. and Fahy, T.J. (1983) Suicide rates in Ireland. *Psychological Medicine, 13,* 385–91.

Cohen, S. and Wills, T. (1985) Stress, social support, and the buffering hypothesis. *Psychological Bulletin, 98,* 310–357.

Cohen-Sandler, R., Berman, A.L. and King, R.A. (1982) A follow-up of hospitalized suicidal children. *Journal of the American Academy of Child Psychiatry, 21,* 398–403.

Coll, X., Law, F., Tobias, A. and Hawton, K. (1998) Child sexual abuse in women who take overdoses: I. A study of prevalence and severity. *Archives of Suicide Research, 4,* 291–306.

Copeland, J.R., Gurland, B.J., Dewey, M.E., Kelleher, M.J., Smith, A.M. and Davidson, I.A. (1987) Is there more dementia, depression and neurosis in New York? A comparative study of the elderly in New York and London using a computer diagnosis AGECAT. *British Journal of Psychiatry, 151,* 466–473.

Crombie, I.K. (1990a) Can changes in the unemployment rates explain the recent changes in suicide rates in developed countries? *International Journal of Epidemiology, 19,* 412–416.

Crombie, I.K. (1990b) Suicide in England and Wales and in Scotland: An examination of divergent trends. *British Journal of Psychiatry, 157,* 529–532.

Cummings, P., Koepsell, T.D., Grossman, D.C. et al. (1997) The association between the purchase of a handgun and homicide or suicide. *American Journal of Public Health, 87*, 974–978.

Dalgard, O.S., Bjork, S. and Tambs, K. (1995) Social support, negative life events and mental health. *British Journal of Psychiatry, 166*, 29–34.

Daly, M. and Kelleher, M.J. (1987) The increase in the suicide rate in Ireland. *Irish Medical Journal, 80*, 233–234.

Darbonne, A.R. (1969) Suicide and age: a suicide note analysis. *Journal of Consulting and Clinical Psychology, 33*, 1, 46–50.

Daub, D. (1992) Death as a release in the Bible. In *The Anchor Bible Dictionary*, Vol. 6. London: Doubleday.

Davidson, K. and Tyrer, P. (1996) Cognitive therapy for antisocial and borderline personality disorder: A single case study series. *British Journal of Clinical Psychology, 35*, 413–429.

Davies, J.B. (1997) *The Myth of Addiction.* Reading: Harwood Academic.

De Boissant, B.A. (1856) *Du suicide et de la Folie suicide consideres dans leurs rapports avec la statistique, la medecine et la philosophe.* Paris: Germer Bailliere.

DeVanna, M., Paterniti, S., Milevich, C., Rigamonti, R., Sulich, A. and Faravelli, C. (1990) Recent life events and attempted suicide. *Journal of Affective Disorders, 18*, 51–58.

Diamoud, G.M., More, L., Hawkins, A.G. and Soucar, E. (1995) Comment on Black's (1993) article 'Comparing genuine and simulated suicidal notes: a new perspective'. *Journal of Consulting and Clinical Psychology, 63*, 1, 46–48.

Diekstra, R.F.W. (1990) Suicide, depression, and economic conditions. In D. Lester (Ed.) *Current Concepts in Suicide.* Philadelphia: Charles Press.

Diekstra, R.F.W. (1993) The epidemiology of suicide and parasuicide. *Acta Psychiatrica Scandinavica*, suppl. *371*, 9–20.

Diekstra, R.F.W. (1994) On the burden of suicide. In M.J Kelleher (Ed.) *Divergent Perspectives on Suicidal Behaviour.* Fifth European Symposium on Suicide. Cork: O'Leary Ltd.

Dorpat, T. and Riley, H. (1960) A study of suicide in the Seattle area. *Comprehensive Psychiatry, 1*, 349–359.

Douglas, J.D. (1967) *The Social Meanings of Suicide.* Princeton, N.J.: Princeton University Press.

Durkheim, E. (1897) *Le Suicide.* Paris (translated by J.A. Spaulding and C. Simpson, 1952) as *Suicide: A Study of Sociology.* London: Routledge and Kegan Paul.

Elliott, A.J., Pages, K.P., Russo, J., Wilson, L.G. and Roy-Byrne, P.P. (1996) *Journal of Clinical Psychiatry, 57* , 567–571.

Ellis, S.J. and Walsh, S. (1986) Soap may seriously damage your health. *Lancet, 8549*, 686.

Engel, G.L. (1980) The clinical application of the biopsychosocial model. *American Journal of Psychiatry, 137*, 535–544.

Erikson, C. (1968) *Identity: Youth and Crisis.* New York: Norton.

Esquirol, E. (1838) Des maladies mentales considerée sous les rapports médical, hygienique et médico-legal. Paris: Bailliere.

Evans, K., Tyrer, P., Catalan, J., Schmidt, U., Davidson, K., Dent, J., Tata, P., Thornton, S., Barber, J. and Thompson, S. (1999) Manual-assisted cognitive-behaviour therapy (MACT): a randomised controlled trial of a brief intervention with bibliotherapy in the treatment of recurrent deliberate self-harm. *Psychological Medicine, 29*, 19–25.

Falret, J.P. (1982) *De l'Hypochondrie et du Suicide*. Paris: Croullebois.

FerradaNoli, M. (1997) A cross-cultural breakdown of Swedish suicide. *Acta Psychiatrica Scandinavica, 96*, 108–116.

Firestone, L. and Seiden, R.H. (1992) Suicide and the continuum of self-destructive behaviours. *Proceedings of the Harvard Medical School, 55–57*.

Foster, T., Gillespie, K. and McClelland, R. (1997) Mental disorders and suicide in Northern Ireland. *British Journal of Psychiatry, 170*, 447–452.

Fowler, R.C., Tsuang, M.T. and Kronfol, Z. (1979) Communication of suicidal intent and suicide in unipolar depression. A forty year follow-up. *Journal of Affective Disorders, 1*, 219–225.

Freud, S. (1905/1974) Fragments of an analysis of a case of hysteria.In J. Strachey (Ed. and trans.). *The Standard Edition of the Complete Psychological Works of Sigmund Freud*, Vol VI. London: Hogarth Press.

Freud, S. (1920) 'A case of homosexuality in a woman'. In J. Strachey (Ed. and trans.). *The Standard Edition of the Complete Psychological Works of Sigmund Freud*, Vol XVIII, pp. 147–172. London: Hogarth Press.

Friedman, R., Corn, R., Hurt, S., Fibel, B., Schulick, J. and Swirsky, S. (1984) Family history of illness in the seriously suicidal adolescent: A life-cycle approach. *American Journal of Orthopsychiatry, 54*, 390–397.

Gallagher, A.G. and Sheehy, N.P. (1994) Suicide in rural communities. *Journal of Community and Applied Social Psychology, 4*, 145–155.

Garzotto, N., Siani, R., Tansella, C.Z. and Tansella, M. (1976) Cross-validation of a predictive scale for subsequent suicidal behaviour in an Italian sample. *British Journal of Psychiatry, 128*, 137–140.

Gilliland, D. (1995) Research note: an attempt to classify adolescent parasuicide attempters. *British Journal of Social Work, 25*, 647–657.

Goodwin, F.K. and Jamison, K.R. (1990) *Manic-depressive Illness*. New York: Oxford University Press.

Gould, M.S. (1990) Suicide clusters and media exposure. In S.J. Blumenthal and D.J. Kupfer (Eds) *Suicide Over the Life Cycle: Risk Factors, Assessment and Treatment of Suicidal Patients*. Washington DC: American Psychiatric Press.

Gunnell, D. and Frankel, S. (1994) Prevention of suicide: Aspirations and evidence. *British Medical Journal, 308*, 1227–1233.

Gupta, K., Sivakumar, K. and Smeeton, N. (1995) Deliberate self-harm: a comparison of first-time cases and cases with a prior history. *Irish Journal of Psychological Medicine, 12* ,131–133.

Guze, S. and Robins, E. (1970) Suicide and primary affective disorder. *British Journal of Psychiatry, 117*, 437–438.

Hamachek, D.E. (1978) Psychodynamics of normal and neurotic perfectionism. *Psychology, 15,* 27–33.

Harris, E.C. and Barraclough, B. (1997) Suicide as an outcome for mental disorders: A meta-analysis. *British Journal of Psychiatry, 170,* 205–228.

Harris, T.E. and Lennings, C.J. (1993) Suicide and adolescence. *International Journal of Offender Therapy and Comparative Criminology, 37,* 263–270.

Hassan, R. (1998) Durkheim oration: Durkheim and Australian suicidology. In R.J Kosky et al. *Suicide Prevention.* New York: Plenum Press.

Hawton, K. (1987) Assessment of suicide risk. *British Journal of Psychiatry, 150,* 145–153.

Hawton, K. (1992) By their own hand. *British Medical Journal, 304,* 1000.

Hawton, K. (1994) Suicidal behaviours in young people: current issues. In M.J. Kelleher, (Ed.) *Divergent Perspectives on Suicidal Behaviour.* Fifth European Symposium on Suicide. Cork: O'Leary Ltd.

Hawton, K. and Fagg, J. (1992) Trends in deliberate self-poisoning and self-injury in Oxford, 1976–1990. *British Medical Journal, 304,* 1409–1411.

Hawton, K., Fagg, J., Platt, S. and Hawkins, M. (1993) Factors associated with suicide after parasuicide in young people. *British Medical Journal, 304,* 1409–1411.

Hawton, K., Fagg, J., Simkin, S., Harriss, L. and Malmberg, A. (1998) Methods used for suicide by farmers in England and Wales. The contribution of availability and its relevance to prevention. *British Journal of Psychiatry, 173,* 320–324.

Hawton, K., Haigh, R., Simkin, S. and Fagg, J. (1995) Attempted suicide in Oxford University students, 1976–1990. *Psychological Medicine, 25,* 179–188.

Hawton, K. and Kirk, J. (1989) Problem-solving treatment. In K. Hawton, D. Clark, P. Salkovskis and J. Kirk (Eds) *Cognitive Therapy for Adult Psychiatric Patients.* Oxford: Oxford University Press.

Hawton, K., Simkin, S., Deeks, J., O'Connor, S., Keen, A., Altman, D., Philo, G. and Bulstrode, C. (1999) Effects of a drug overdose in a television drama on presentations to hospital for self poisoning: time series and questionnaire study. *British Medical Journal, 318,* 972–977.

Hawton, K., Ware, C., Mistry, H., Hewitt, J., Kingsbury, S., Roberts, D. and Weitzel, H. (1996) Paracetamol self-poisoning. Characteristics, prevention and harm reduction. *British Journal of Psychiatry, 168,* 43–48.

Hendin, H. (1982) *Suicide in America.* New York: Norton.

Henry, A.F. and Short, J.F. (1954) *Suicide and Homicide.* New York: Free Press.

Hewitt, P.L.and Flett, G.L. (1991) Perfectionism in the self and social contexts: Conceptualization, assessment, and association with psychopathology, *Journal of Personaliy and Social Psychology, 60,* 456–470.

Home Office Working Group on Suicide Prevention. London: HMSO.

Irish Government Publications Office (1998) Final Report of the National Task Force on Suicide. Dublin: Irish Government Publications.

Jacobs, J. (1971) *Adolescent Suicide.* New York: Wiley Interscience.

Jamison, S. (1997) *Assisted Suicide.* San Francisco: Jossey-Bass.

Jobes, D.A., Berman, A.L. and Josselon, A.R. (1986) The impact of psychological autopsies on medical examiners' determination of manner of death. *Journal of Forensic Sciences, 31,* 177–189.

Johansson, L.M., Sundquist, J., Johansson, S.E., Bergman, B., Qvist, J. and Traskman-Bendz, L. (1997) Suicide among foreign-born minorities and native Swedes: An epidemiological follow-up of a defined population. *Social Science and Medicine, 44,* 181–187.

Kelleher, M.J. (1991) Suicide in Ireland. *Irish Medical Journal, 84,* 40–41.

Kelleher, M.J. (1998) Youth suicide trends in the Republic of Ireland. *British Journal of Psychiatry, 172,* 196–97.

Kelleher, M.J., Corcoran, P., Keeley, H.S., Dennehy, J. and O'Donnell, I. (1996) Improving procedures for recording suicide statistics. *Irish Medical Journal, 89,* 14–15.

Kelleher, M.J. and Daly, M. (1990) Suicide in Cork and Ireland. *British Journal of Psychiatry, 157,* 533–538.

Kelleher, M.J., Daly, M., Keohane, B., Daly, C., Daly, F., Crowley, M. and Kelleher, M.J.A. (1994) Deprivation and long term outcome of deliberate self-poisoning. In M. Kelleher (Ed.) *Divergent Perspectives on Suicidal Behaviour.* Fifth European Symposium on Suicide. Cork: O'Leary Ltd.

Kelly, D. and France, R. (1987) *A Practical Handbook for the Treatment of Depression.* Carnforth: Parthenon.

Kessel, N. and Grossman, G. (1961) Suicide in Alcoholism. *British Medical Journal, 2,* 1671–1672.

Knights, A., Okasha, M., Salih, M. and Hirsch, S. (1979) Depressive and extrapyramidal symptoms and clinical effects. *British Journal of Psychiatry, 135,* 515–523.

Kosky, R.J., Eshkevari, H.S., Goldney, R.D. and Hassan, R. (1998) *Suicide Prevention: The Global Context.* New York: Kluwer Academic.

Kreitman, N. (1976) The coal gas story: UK suicide rates 1960–71. *British Journal of Preventive and Social Medicine, 30,* 86–93.

Kreitman, N. (1977) *Parasuicide.* Chichester: Wiley.

Kreitman, N. (1986) The clinical assessment and management of the suicidal patient. In A. Roy (Ed.) *Suicide.* Baltimore: Williams and Wilkins.

Kreitman, N. and Foster, J. (1991) The construction and selection of predictive scales with particular reference to parasuicide. *British Journal of Psychiatry, 159,* 185–192.

Kuhse, H. (1987) *The Sanctity of Life Doctrine in Medicine: A Critique.* Oxford: Clarendon Press.

Kurz, A., Moller, H.J., Baindl, G., Burk, F., Torhorstm, A., Wachtler, C. and Lauter, H. (1987) Classification of parasuicide by cluster analysis. Types of suicidal behaviour, therapeutic and prognostic implications. *British Journal of Psychiatry, 150,* 520-525.

Lachaise, C. (1822) *Topographie medicale de Paris.* Paris: Bailliere.

Langley, G. and Bayatti, N. (1974) Suicide in Exe Vale Hospital 1972–1981. *British Journal of Psychiatry, 145,* 463–467.

Law, F., Coll, X., Tobias, A. and Hawton, K. (1998) Child sexual abuse in women who take overdoses: II. Risk factors and associations. *Archives of Suicide Research, 4,* 307–327.

Leenaars, A. (1979) A study of the manifest content of suicide notes from three different theoretical perspectives: L. Binswanger, S. Freud and G. Kelly. Unpublished Ph.D. Dissertation. University of Windsor, Windsor, Canada.

Leenaars, A. (1987) An empirical investigation of Shneidman's formulations regarding suicide: Age and sex. *Suicide and Life-threatening Behaviour, 17,* 233–250.

Leenaars, A. (1988a) *Suicide Notes.* New York: Human Sciences Press.

Leenaars, A. (1988b) Are women's suicides really different from men's? *Women and Health, 18,* 17–33.

Leenaars, A. (1989) Suicide across the adult lifespan: An archival study. *Crisis, 10,* 132–151.

Leenaars, A. (1992) Suicide notes, communication and ideation. In R.W. Maris, A.L. Berman, J.T. Maltsberger and R.I. Yufit *Assesssment and Prediction of Suicide.* New York: Guilford Press.

Leenaars, A. (1996) Suicide: a multidimensional malaise. *Suicide and Life-threatening Behavior, 26,* 221–235.

Leenaars, A.A. and Balance, W.D.G. (1984a) A logical empirical approach to the study of suicide notes. *Canadian Journal of Behavioural Science, 16,* 249–256.

Leenaars, A. and Balance, W. (1984b) A predictive approach to Freud's formulations regarding suicide. *Suicide and Life-threatening Behaviour, 14,* 275–283.

Lehtinen, V., Joukamaa, M. and Jyrkinen, E. et al (1990) Need for mental health services of the population in Finland: Results from a mini Finland Health Survey. *Acta Psychiatrica Scandinavica, 81,* 426–431.

Lester, D. (1989a) National suicide and homicide rates: Correlates versus predictors. *Social Science and Medicine, 29,* 1249–1252.

Lester, D. (1989b) *Can We Prevent Suicide?* New York: AMS Press.

Lester, D. (1998) Adolescent suicide risk today: a paradox. *Journal of Adolescence, 21,* 449–503.

Lester, D. and Heim, N. (1992) Sex differences in suicide notes. *Perceptual and Motor Skills, 75,* 582.

Lester, D. and Hummel, H. (1980) Motives for suicide in elderly people. *Psychological Reports, 47,* 870.

Lester, D. and Murrell, M. (1980) The influence of gun control laws on suicidal behaviour. *American Journal of Psychiatry, 38,* 121–122.

Lester, D. and Reeve, C. (1982) The suicide notes of young and old people. *Psychological Reports, 50,* 334.

Lewis, G., Hawton, K. and Jones, P. (1997) Strategies for preventing suicide. *British Journal of Psychiatry, 171,* 351–354.

Lewis, G. and Sloggett, A. (1998) Suicide, deprivation, and unemployment: record linkage study. *British Medical Journal, 3,* 1283–1286.

Linehan, M.M., Camper, P., Chiles, J.A., Strohsak, K. and Shearin, E.N. (1987) Interpersonal problem-solving and parasuicide. *Cognitive Therapy and Research, 11,* 1–2.

Linehan, M., Heard, H.L. and Armstrong, H.E. (1993) Naturalistic follow-up of a behavioural treatment for chronically parasuicidal borderline clients. *Archives of General Psychiatry, 50,* 971–974.

Litman, R.E. (1994) Long-term treatment of chronically suicidal patients. In E.S. Shneidman, N.L. Farberow and R.E. Litman. *The Psychology of Suicide: A Clinician's Guide to Evaluation and Treatment.* New York: Jason Aronson.

MacLeod, A.K., Pankhania, B., Lee, M. and Mitchell, D. (1997) Parasuicide, depression and the anticipation of positive and negative future expectations. *Psychological Medicine, 27,* 973–977.

MacLeod, A.K., Rose, G.S. and Williams, J.M.G. (1993) Components of hoplessness about the future in parasuicide. *Cognitive Therapy and Research, 17,* 5, 441–445.

MacLeod, A., Tata, P., Evans, K.. Tyrer, P., Schmidt, U., Davidson, K., Thornton, S. and Catalan, J. (1998) Recovery of positive future thinking within a high-risk parasuicide group: Results from a pilot randomized controlled trial. *British Journal of Clinical Psychology, 37,* 371–379.

MacLeod, A.K., Williams, J.M.G. and Linehan, M.M. (1992) New developments in the understanding and treatment of suicidal behaviour. *Behavioural Psychotherapy, 20,* 193–218.

Maris, R.F.W. (1991) Introduction to a special issue: Assessment and prediction of suicide. *Suicide and Life-threatening Behavior, 21,* 1–17.

Maris, R.W. (1994) The prediction of suicide. In M.J. Kelleher (Ed.) *Divergent Perspectives on Suicidal Behaviour.* Fifth European Symposium on Suicide. Cork: O'Leary Ltd.

Marttunen, M.J., Hillevi, M.A., Henriksson, M.M. and Lonnquist, J.K. (1991) Mental disorders in adolescent suicide. DSM-III-R Axes I and II diagnoses in suicides among 13 to 19 year olds in Finland. *Archives of General Psychiatry, 48,* 834-839.

Matarazzo, J.D. (1980) Behavioral health and behavioral medicine. Frontiers for a new health psychology. *American Scientist, 35,* 807–817.

McAuliffe, C. (1998). Suicidal Ideation: An exploration of attitudes to suicidal behavior and problem solving skills. Unpublished MPhil dissertation, University College Cork, Cork, Ireland.

McCarthy, P. and Walsh, D. (1975) Suicide in Dublin: I Under-reporting of suicide and the consequences for national statistics. *British Journal of Psychiatry, 126,* 301–308.

McCrea, P. (1996) Trends in suicide in Northern Ireland 1922–1992. *Irish Journal of Psychological Medicine, 13,* 9–12.

McGorry, P., Henry, L. and Power, P. (1998) Suicide in Early Psychosis. Could early intervention work? In R.J.Kosky, H.S. Eshkevari, R.D. Goldney and R. Hassan (Eds) *Suicide Prevention. The Global Context.* New York: Plenum Press.

McLoone, P. and Crombie (1987) Trends in suicide in Scotland 1974–84: An increasing problem. *British Medical Journal, 295,* 629.

Michel, K. (1986) Suizide und Suizidversuche. *Schweizerische Medizinische Wochenschrift, 116,* 770–774.

Michel, K. and Valach, I. (1992) Suicide prevention: spreading the gospel to general practioners. *British Journal of Psychiatry, 160,* 757–760

Michel, K., Valach, I. and Waeber, V. (1994) Understanding deliberate self-harm: The patients' view. *Crisis, 15,* 172–178.

Miles, C.P. (1977) Conditions predisposing to suicide: a review. *The Journal of Nervous and Mental Disease, 164,* 231–246.

Murphy, G.E. (1986) The physican's role in suicide prevention. In A. Roy (Ed.) *Suicide.* Baltimore: Williams and Wilkins.

Murphy, G.E., Wetzel, R.D., Robins, E. and McEvoy, L. (1992) Multiple risk factors predict suicide in alcoholism. *Archives of General Psychiatry, 49,* 459–463.

Naroll, R. (1969) Cultural determinants and the concept of the sick society. In *Changing Perspectives in Mental Illness.* S.C. Plog and R.B Edgerton. (Eds) New York: Holt, Rinehart and Winston.

Neeleman, J., Halpern, D., Leon, D. and Lewis, G. (1997) Tolerance of suicide, religion and suicide rates: an ecological and individual study in 19 Western countries. *Psychological Medicine, 27,* 1165–1171.

Nordentoft, M. and Rubin, P. (1993) Mental illness and social integration among suicide attempters in Copenhagen. *Acta Psychiatrica Scandinavica, 52,* 81–106.

Noreik, K. (1975) Attempted suicide and suicide in functional psychosis. *Acta Psychiatrica Scandinavica, 52,* 81–106.

O'Carroll, P.W., Berman, A.L., Maris, R., Moscicki, E., Tanney, B. and Silverman, M. (1998) Beyond the tower of babel. A nomenclature for suicidology. In R.J.Kosky, H.S. Eshevari, R.D Goldney and R. Hassan (Eds) *Suicide Prevention: The Global Context.* New York: Plenum.

O'Connor, R.C. (1999) The Boundaries: Health Psychology and Suicidal Behaviour. *Health Psychology Update, 36,* 4–7.

O'Connor, R.C. and Sheehy, N.P. (1997) Suicide and Gender. *Mortality, 2,* 239–254.

O'Connor, R.C., Sheehy, N.P. and O'Connor, D.B. (1999a) A Thematic Suicide Note Analysis: Some observations on depression and previous attempt. *Crisis. 20, 3,* 106–114

O'Connor, R.C., Sheehy, N.P. and O'Connor, D.B. (1999b) A classification of completed suicide into sub-types. *Journal of Mental Health, 8, 6,* 629–637.

O'Connor, R.C., Sheehy, N.P. and O'Connor, D.B. (2000) Fifty cases of general hospital parasuicide. *British Journal of Health Psychology, 5* (in press).

O'Donnell, I. and Farmer, R. (1995) The limitations of official statistics. *British Journal of Psychiatry, 166,* 458–461.

Ogden, J. (1996) *Health Psychology: A Textbook.* Buckingham: Open University Press.

Oglivie, D., Stone, P. and Shneidman, E. (1969) Some characteristics of genuine versus simulated suicide notes. *Bulletins of Suicidology,* March, 17–26.

Orbach, I., Rosenheim, E. and Hary, E. (1987) Some aspects of cognitive functioning in suicidal children. *Journal of American Academy of Child and Adolescent Psychiatry, 26,* 181–185.

141

Ovuga, E. and Mugisha, R. (1990) Attitudes and psychological characteristics of suicidal individuals. *Crisis, 11*, 60–72.

Owens, D., Dennis, M., Read, S. and Davis, N. (1994) Outcome of deliberate self-poisoning. An examination of risk factors for repetition. *British Journal of Psychiatry, 165*, 797–801.

Pacht, A.R. (1984) Reflections on perfection. *American Psychologist, 39*, 386–390.

Paris, J, Brown, R. and Nowlis, D. (1987) Long-term follow-up of borderline personality patients in a general hospital. *Comprehensive Psychiatry, 25*, 530–535.

Paykel, E.S., Prusoff, B.A. and Myers, J.K. (1975) Suicide attempts and recent life events: A controlled comparison. *Archives of General Psychiatry, 32*, 327–333.

Pearson, V. (1993) Suicide in North and West Devon: a comparative study using coroner's inquest papers. *Journal of Public Health Medicine, 15*, 320–236.

Peterson, C., Semmel, A., von Baeyer, C., Abramson, L., Metalksy, G. and Seligman, M. (1982) The attributional style questionnaire. *Cognitive Therapy and Research, 6*, 287–299.

Peuskens, J., De Hert, M., Cosyns, P., Pieters, G., Theys, P. and Vermote, R. (1997) Suicide among young schizophrenic patients during and after inpatient treatment. *International Journal of Mental Health, 25*, 39–44.

Pfohl, B. and Winokur, G. (1983) The micropsychopathology of hebephrenic/catatonic schizophrenia. *Journal of Nervous and Mental Disorders, 171*, 296–300.

Philips, M. (1986) *A Study of Suicides and Attempted Suicides at HMP Brixton 1973–83*. London: HMP Brixton Department of Psychological Services Report Series 1, Number 24.

Platt, J.J., Spivack, G. and Bloom, W. (1975) *Manual for the Means–End Problem-solving Procedure (MEPS): A Measure of Interpersonal Problem-Solving Skill.* Philadephia: Hahnemann Medical College and Hospital, Department of Mental Health Sciences, Hahnemann Community MH/MR Center.

Platt, S. (1984) Unemployment and suicidal behaviour: A review of the literature. *Social Science Medicine, 19* , 93–115.

Platt, S. (1986a) Epidemiology of suicide and parasuicide. *Journal of Psychopharmacology, 6*, 291–299.

Platt, S. (1986b) Suicide and parasuicide among further education students in Edinburgh. *British Journal of Psychiatry, 150*, 183–188.

Platt, S. (1987) The aftermath of Angie's overdose: Is soap (opera) damaging to your health? *British Medical Journal, 294*, 954–957.

Platt, S., (1993) The social transmission of parasuicide: Is there a modelling effect? *Crisis, 14*, 23–31.

Platt, S., Hawton, K., Kreitman, N., Fagg, J. and Foster, J. (1988) Recent clinical and epidemiological trends in parasuicide in Edinburgh and Oxford: A tale of two cities. *Psychological Medicine, 18*, 405–418.

Platt, S. and Kreitman, N. (1984) Trends in parasuicide and unemployment among men in Edinburgh, 1968–82. *British Medical Journal, 289,* 1029–1032.

Platt, S., Micciolo, R. and Tansella, M. (1992) Suicide and unemployment in Italy: A description, analysis and interpretation of recent trends. *Social Science Medicine, 34,* 1191–1201.

Pokorny, A.D. (1983) Suicide prediction revisited. *Suicide and Life-threatening Behaviour, 23,* 1–10.

Pokorny, A.D. (1993) Prediction of suicide in psychiatric patients: report of a prospective study. *Archives of General Psychiatry, 40,* 249–257.

Posener, J.A., LaHaye, A. and Cheifetz, P.N. (1989) Suicide notes in adolescence. *Canadian Journal of Psychiatry, 34,* 171–176.

Poteet, D.J. (1987) Adolescent suicide: A review of 87 cases of completed suicide in Shelby County, Tennessee. *The American Journal of Forensic Medicine and Pathology, 8 ,* 12–17.

Power, K., Davies, C., Swanson, V., Gordon, D. and Carter, H. (1997) Case-control study of GP attendance rates by suicide cases with or without a psychiatric history. *British Journal of General Practice, 47,* 211– 215.

Priest, R.G. (1991) A new initiative on depresssion. *British Journal of General Practice, 41,* 487.

Priest, R.G. (1994) Improving the management and knowledge of depression. *British Journal of Psychiatry, 164,* 285–287.

Priester, M.J. and Clum, G.A. (1993) The problem-solving diathesis in depression, hopelessness and suicidal ideation: A longitudinal analysis. *Journal of Psychopathology and Behavioural Assessment, 15,* 239–254.

Rachels, J. (1986) *The End of Life: Euthanasia and Morality.* Oxford: Oxford University Press.

Register General for Northern Ireland (1992) *Register General's Report for Northern Ireland.* Belfast: HMSO.

Rennie, T.A.C. (1939) Follow-up study of 500 patients with schizophrenia admitted to the hospital from 1913–1923. *Archives of Neurology and Psychiatry, 42,* 877–891.

Roberts. J. and Hawton. K. (1980) Child abuse and attempted suicide. *British Journal of Psychiatry, 137,* 319–323.

Robin, A. and Freeman-Bawne, D. (1968) Drugs left at home by psychiatric patients. *British Medical Journal, 3,* 424–425.

Robins, E., Murphy, G., Wilkinson, R., Gassner, S. and Kayes, J. (1959) Some clinical considerations in the prevention of suicide based on a study of 134 successful suicides. *American Journal of Public Health, 49,* 888–898.

Rockwell, D.A. and O'Brien, W. (1973) Physicans' knowledge and attitudes to suicide. *Journal of American Medical Association, 225,* 1347–1349.

Rodger, C.R. and Scott, A.I.F. (1995) Frequent deliberate self-harm – repetition, suicide and cost after 3 years. *Scottish Medical Journal, 40,* 10–12.

Rogers, J.R. and Carney, J.V. (1994) Assessing the 'Modeling Effect' in parasuicidal behaviour: A comment on Platt (1993). *Crisis, 15,* 83–89.

Rosenberg, M.L., Davidson, L.E., Smith, J.C., Berman, A.L., Buzbee, H., Gantner, G., Gay, G.A., Moore-Lewis, B., Mills, D.H., Murray, D., O'Carroll,

P.W. and Jobes, D. (1988) Operational criteria for the determination of suicide. *Journal of Forensic Sciences*, 32, 1445–1455.

Rotherman-Borus, M.J. Trautman, P., Dopkins, S. and Shrout, P. (1990) Cognitive style and pleasant activities among female adolescent suicide attempters. *Journal of Consulting and Clinical Psychology*, 58, 554–561.

Roy, A. (1982a) Risk factors for suicide in psychiatric patients. *Archives of General Psychiatry*, 39, 1089–1095.

Roy, A. (1982b Suicide in Chronic Schizophrenia. *British Journal of Psychiatry*, 141, 171–177.

Roy, A. and Linnoila, M. (1986) Alcoholism and suicide. In R.W. Maris (Ed.) *Biology of Suicide*. New York: Guilford Press.

Runeson, B. (1989) Mental disorder in youth suicide – DSM III-R Axes I and Axes II. *Acta Psychiatrica Scandinavica*, 79, 490–497.

Runeson, B. and Beskow, J. (1991) Borderline personality disorder in young Swedish suicides. *Journal of Nervous and Mental Disease*, 179, 153–156.

Rutz, L., von Knorring, L. and Walinder, J. (1989) Frequency of suicide on Gotland after systematic postgraduate education of general practitioners. *Acta Psychiatrica Scandinavica*, 80, 151–154.

Rutz, L., von Knorring, L. and Walinder, J. (1992) Long term effects of an educational programme for general practitioners given by the Swedish Committee for the Prevention and Treatment of Depression. *Acta Psychiatrica Scandinavica*, 85, 83–88.

Sainsbury, P. (1986) Depression, suicide and suicide prevention. In A. Roy (Ed.) *Suicide*. Baltimore: Williams and Wilkins.

Sainsbury, P. (1955) *Suicide in London*. London: Chapman and Hall.

Sainsbury, P. and Barraclough, B. (1968) Differences between suicide rates. *Nature*, 220, 1252.

Sakinofsky, I., Roberts, R., Brown, Y., Cunning, C. and James, P. (1990) Proper resolution and repetition of parasuicide: a prospective study. *British Journal of Psychiatry*, 156, 395–399.

Salkovskis, P., Atha, C. and Storer, D. (1990) Cognitive-behavioural problem-solving in the treatment of patients who repeatedly attempt suicide. A controlled trial. *British Journal of Psychiatry*, 157, 871–876.

Schotte, D.E and Clum, G.A (1982) Suicide ideation in a college population – a test of a model. *Journal of Consulting and Clinical Psychology*, 50, 5, 690-696.

Schotte, D. and Clum, G. (1987) Problem-solving skills in suicidal psychiatric patients. *Journal of Consulting and Clinical Psychology*, 55, 49–54.

Schynder, U. and Valach, L. (1997) Suicide attempters in a psychiatric emergency room population. *General Hospital Psychiatry*, 19, 119–129.

Secretary of State for Health (1992) *The Health of the Nation*. London: HMSO.

Seligman, M.E.P. and Maier, S.F. (1967) The failure to escape traumatic shock. *Journal of Experimental Psychology*, 74, 1–9.

Serin, S. (1926) Une enquete medico-psychologique sur le suicide à Paris. *La Presse Medicale*, November, 1404–1406.

Shaffer, D., Garland, A., Gould, M., Fisher, P., Trautman, P. (1988) Preventing teenage suicide: a critical review. *Journal of American Academy of Child and Adolescent Psychiatry, 27*, 675–687.

Shaffer, D., Gould, M. and Hicks, R. (1994) Epidemiology, mechanisms and clinical features of youth suicide. In M.J. Kelleher (Ed.) *Divergent Perspectives on Suicidal Behaviour*. Fifth European Symposium on Suicide. Cork: O'Leary Ltd.

Shafii, M., Steltz-Lenarsky, J., Derrik, A M., Beckner, C., and Whittinghill, J.R. (1988) Comorbidity of mental disorders in the post-mortem diagnosis of completed suicide in children and adolescents. *Journal of Affective Disorders, 15*, 233–277.

Shepherd, D. and Barraclough, B. (1980) Work and suicide: an empirical investigation. *British Journal of Psychiatry, 136*, 469–478.

Shneidman E. S. (1973) *Deaths of Man*. New York: Jason Aronson Inc.

Shneidman, E.S. (1980) *Voices of Man*. New York: Harper and Row.

Shneidman, E.S. (1981) The psychological autopsy. *Suicide and Life-threatening Behaviour, 11*, 325–340.

Shneidman, E.S. (1985) *Definition of Suicide*. New York: John Wiley and Sons.

Shneidman, E.S. (1986) Some essentials for suicide and some implications for response. In Roy, A. (Ed.) *Suicide*. Baltimore: Williams and Wilkins.

Shneidman, E.S. (1988) In A.A. Leenaars *(Ed.) Suicide Notes. Predictive Clues and Patterns*. New York: Human Sciences Press Inc.

Shneidman, E.S. (1996) *The Suicidal Mind*. New York: Oxford University Press.

Shneidman, E.S. and Farberow, N.L. (1957) *Clues to Suicide*. New York: McGraw-Hill.

Shneidman, E.S. and Farberow, N. (1960) A socio-psychological investigation of suicide. In H.P. David and J.C. Brengelmann (Eds) *Perspectives in Personality Research*. New York: Springer.

Shrieber, T.J. and Johnson, R.L. (1986) The evaluation and treatment of adolescent overdoses in an adolescent medical service. *Journal of the National Medical Association, 78*, 101–108.

Siani, R., Garzotto, N., Tansella, C.Z. and Tansella, M. (1979) Predictive scales for parasuicide repetition. *Acta Psychiatrica Scandinavica, 59*, 17–23.

Spirito, A., Brown, L., Overholser, J. and Fritz, G. (1989) Attempted suicide in adolescence: a review and critique of the literature. *Clinical Psychology Review, 9*, 335–363.

Spirito, A., Sterling, C.M., Donaldson, D.L. and Arrigan, M.E. (1996) Factor analysis of the suicide intent scale with adolescent attempters. *Journal of Personality Assessment, 67*, 90–101.

Spurzheim, J.G. (1818) *Observations sur la folie, ou sur les derangemens des fonctions morales et intellectuelles de l'homme*, pp. 207–20. Paris: Treuttel and Wurtz.

Stanley, E. J. and Baxter, J.J. (1970) Adolecent suicidal behaviour. *American Journal of Orthopsychiatry, 40*, 87–96.

Stengel, E. (1964) *Suicide and Attempted Suicide*. Baltimore: Penguin Books.

Stoney, G. (1998) Suicide Prevention on the internet. In R.J.Kosky, H.S

Eshkevari, R.D. Goldney and R. Hassan (Eds) *Suicide Prevention: The Global Context*. New York: Plenum Press.

Stuhmuller, Carroll (Ed,) (1996) *The Collegiate Pastoral Dictionary of Biblical Theology*. Minnesota: Liturgical Press.

Suokas, J. and Lonnqvist, J. (1991) Outcome of attempted suicide and psychiatric consultation: risk factors and suicide mortality during a five year follow-up. *Acta Psychiatica Scandinavica, 84*, 545–549.

Taylor, S. (1982) *Durkheim and the Study of Suicide*. London: Macmillan.

Taylor, R., Morrell, S., Slaytor, E. and Ford, P. (1998) Suicide in urban New South Wales, Australia 1985–1994: Socio-economic and migrant interactions. *Social Science and Medicine, 47*, 1677–1686.

Teicher, J.D. (1970) Children and adolescents who attempt suicide. *Pediatric Clinics of North America, 17*, 687–696.

Topp, D.O. (1979) Suicide in prisons. *British Journal of Psychiatry, 134*, 24–27.

Traskman-Bendz, L., Allig, C., Oreland, L., Regnell, G., Vinge, E. and Ohman, R. (1991) Prediction of suicidal behaviour from biologic tests. *Journal of Clinical Psychopharmocology, 12*, 21S-26S.

Tripodes, P. (1976) Reasoning patterns in suicide notes. In E. Shneidman (Ed.) *Suicidology: Contemporary Developments*. New York: Grune and Stratton.

Tuckman, J., Kleiner, R.J. and Lavell, M. (1959) Emotional content of suicide notes. *American Journal of Psychiatry, 116*, 59–63.

van der Maas, P.J., van Delden, J.J.M., Pijnenborg, L. and Looman, C.W.N. (1991) Euthanasia and other medical decisions concerning the end of life. *The Lancet, 338*, 669–674.

van der Maas, P.J., van der Wal, G., Haverkate, I., de Graaf, C.L.M., Kester, J.G.C., Onwuteaka-Philipsen, B.D., van der Heide, A., Bosma, J.M. and Willems, D.M. (1996) Euthanasia, physician-assisted suicide, and other medical practices involving the end of life in the Netherlands, 1990–1995. *The New England Journal of Medicine, 335*, 1699–1705.

van der Wal, G., van Eijk, J.Th.M., Leenen, H.J.J. and Spreeuwenberg, C. (1992) Euthanasia and assisted suicide, I: How often is it practised by family doctors in the Netherlands? *Family Practice, 9*, 130–134.

van der Wal, G., van der Maas, P.J., Bosma, J.M., Onwuteaka-Philipsen, B.D., Willems, D.L., Haverkate, I. and Kostense, P.J. (1996) Evaluation of the notification procedure for physician-assisted death in the Netherlands. *The New England Journal of Medicine, 335*, 1706–1711.

van Hooff, A.J. (1994) Suicide in antiquity: From kin-killing to self-murder. In M.J. Kelleher (Ed.) *Divergent Perspectives on Suicidal Behaviour*. Cork: O'Leary Ltd.

Vassilas, C. and Morgan, H. (1997) Suicide in Avon: Life stress, alcohol misuse, and use of services. *British Journal of Psychiatry, 170*, 453–455.

Virkkunen, M. (1984) Suicide in schizophrenia and paranoid psychosis. *Acta Psychiatrica Scandinavica* (Suppl) *250*, 1–305.

Vlachos, I., Bouras, N., Watson, J. and Rosen, B. (1994) Deliberate self-harm referrals. *European Journal of Psychiatry, 8*, 25–28.

Wagner, F. (1960) Suicide notes. *Danish Medical Journal, 7*, 62–64.

Watanabe, N., Hasegawa, K. and Yoshinaga, Y. (1995) Suicide in later life in Japan: urban and rural differences, *International Psychogeriatrics, 7*, 253–261.

Weeke, A. and Vaeth, M. (1986) Excess mortality of bipolar and unipolar depressive patients. *Journal of Affective Disorders, 11*, 227–234.

Werth Jr, J.L. and Liddle, B.J. (1994) Psychotherapists' attitudes toward suicide. *Psychotherapy: Theory, Research and Practice, 31*, 440–448.

WHO (1986) *Working Group on Preventive Practices in Suicide and Attempted Suicides: Summary Report* (ICP/PSF 017 6525) WHO, Regional Office for Europe, Copenhagen, Denmark.

Williams, J.M.G. (1996a) Depression and the specificity of autobiographical memory. In D.C. Rubin (Ed.) *Remembering Our Past: Studies in Autobiographical Memory*. Cambridge: Cambridge University Press.

Williams, J.M.G. (1996b) *The Psychological Treatment of Depression*. London: Routledge

Williams, J.M.G. (1997) *Cry of Pain*. London: Penguin.

Williams, J.M.G. and Broadbent, K. (1986) Autobiographical memory in attempted suicide patients. *Journal of Abnormal Psychology, 95*, 144–149.

Williams, J.M.G. and Pollock, L.R. (1993) Factors mediating suicidal behaviour: their utility in primary and secondary prevention. *Journal of Mental Health, 2*, 3–26.

Winchel, R., Stanley, B. and Stanley, M. (1990) Biochemical aspects of suicide. In S.J. Blumenthal and D.J. Kupfer (Eds) *Suicide Over the Life Cycle: Risk Factors, Assessment and Treatment of Suicidal Patients*. Washington, DC: American Psychiatric Association Press.

Windle, M., Miller-Tutzauer, C. and Domenico, D. (1992) Alcohol use, suicidal behaviour, and risky activities among adolescents. *Journal of Research on Adolescence, 2*, 317–330.

Winkler, E. (1995) Reflections on the state of current debate over physician-assisted suicide and euthanasia. *Bioethics, 9*, 313–326.

Yang, B. and Clum, G.A. (1994) Life stress, social support and problem-solving skills predictive of depressive symptoms, hopelessness, and suicidal ideation in an Asian student population. *Suicide and Life-threatening Behavior, 24*, 127–139.

Index

Note: Page numbers in *italic* type refer to *tables*